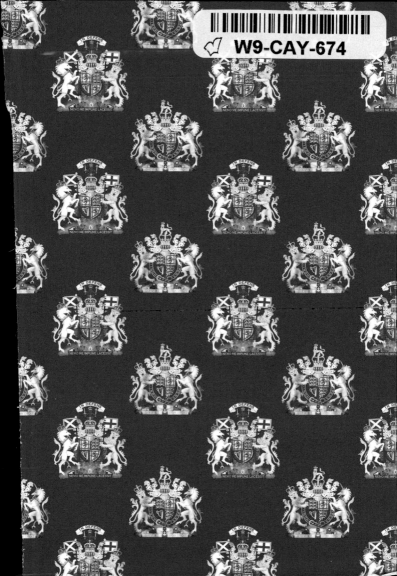

Royal Weddings

A Very Peculiar History™

With added Meghan Markle

'All marriage is such a lottery.'
Queen Victoria (reigned 1837–1901)

For A, with love, as always

FMacD

Editors: Stephen Haynes, Nick Pierce

Cover illustration by: David Lyttleton
Additional artwork by: Shutterstock

Published in Great Britain in MMXVIII by
Book House, an imprint of
The Salariya Book Company Ltd
25 Marlborough Place, Brighton BN1 1UB
www.salariya.com

ISBN: 978-1-912233-96-0

A CIP catalogue record for this book is available
from the British Library.

Printed and bound in Turkey.
Printed on paper from sustainable sources.

Visit
www.salariya.com
for our online catalogue and
free fun stuff.

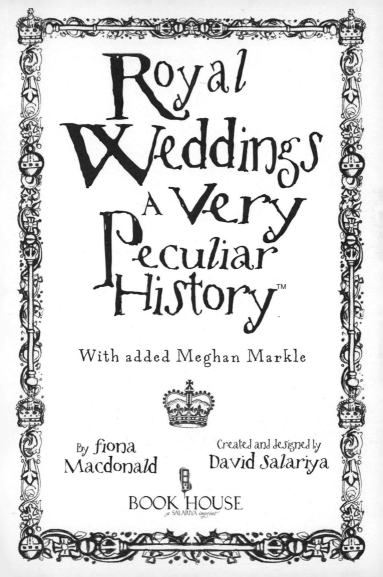

Royal Weddings
A Very Peculiar History™

With added Meghan Markle

By Fiona Macdonald

Created and designed by David Salariya

BOOK HOUSE
a SALARIYA imprint

Q. *Which princess took her favourite corgi on honeymoon with her?*

A. Princess Elizabeth (later Queen Elizabeth II), in 1947.

Q. *Which royal bride put nettles and wild garlic on the menu at her wedding breakfast?*

A. Crown Princess Victoria of Sweden, in 2010.

Q. *Which writer who criticised a royal wedding had his right hand cut off?*

A. Puritan gentleman John Stubbe, in 1579. He protested against Queen Elizabeth I's rumoured plans to wed French King Henry III.

Q. *Which royal couple went without a wedding reception?*

A. Prince Ali of Jordan and his bride, former journalist Rym Brahimi, in 2004. They used the money they saved to buy food for 1000 of Jordan's poorest families.

Contents

Some descendants of Queen Victoria

Victoria = Albert of Saxe-Coburg-Gotha
b. 1819, r. 1837–1901   1819–1861

- **Victoria**
  m. Frederick III of Prussia

- **Edward VII**
  b. 1841, r. 1901–1910
  m. Pr. Alexandra of Denmark

- **Alice**
  m. Ludwig IV grand duke of Hesse

- **Alfred**
  m. Grand Duchess Marie Alexandrovna

- **Helena**
  m. Pr. Christian of Schleswig-Holstein

- **Louise**
  m. 9th duke of Argyll

- **Arthur**
  m. Pr. Louise of Prussia

- **Leopold**
  m. Pr. Helena of Waldeck & Pyrmont

- **Beatrice**
  m. Pr. Henry of Battenburg

Children of Edward VII:

- **Albert Victor**
  duke of Clarence and Avondale

- **George V**
  b. 1865, r. 1910–1936
  m. Pr. Mary of Teck

- **Louise**
  m. 1st duke of Fife

- **Victoria**

- **Maud**
  m. Haakon VII of Norway

- **Alexander**

Children of George V:

- **Edward VIII**
  b. 1894, r. 1936, d. 1986
  m. Wallis Simpson

- **Mary**
  Princess Royal
  m. earl of Harewood

- **George**
  duke of Kent
  m. Pr. Marina of Greece

- **John**

6

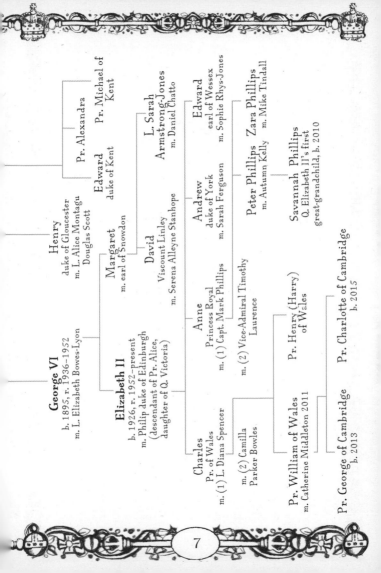

George VI
b. 1895, r. 1936–1952
m. L. Elizabeth Bowes-Lyon

Henry
duke of Gloucester
m. L. Alice Montagu
Douglas Scott

Margaret
m. earl of Snowdon

David
Viscount Linley
m. Serena Alleyne Stanhope

L. Sarah
Armstrong-Jones
m. Daniel Chatto

Pr. Alexandra   Pr. Michael
of Kent

Edward
duke of Kent

Elizabeth II
b. 1926, r. 1952–present
m. Philip duke of Edinburgh
(descendant of Pr. Alice,
daughter of Q. Victoria)

Charles
Pr. of Wales
m. (1) L. Diana Spencer

m. (2) Camilla
Parker Bowles

Anne
Princess Royal
m. (1) Capt. Mark Phillips

m. (2) Vice-Admiral Timothy
Laurence

Andrew
duke of York
m. Sarah Ferguson

Edward
earl of Wessex
m. Sophie Rhys-Jones

Pr. William of Wales
m. Catherine Middleton 2011

Pr. Henry (Harry)
of Wales

Peter Phillips
m. Autumn Kelly

Zara Phillips
m. Mike Tindall

Pr. George of Cambridge
b. 2013

Pr. Charlotte of Cambridge
b. 2015

Savannah Phillips
Q. Elizabeth II's first
great-grandchild, b. 2010

6 A princely marriage
is a brilliant edition
of a universal fact...
and as such, it rivets
mankind. 9

Walter Bagehot (1826–1877)

INTRODUCTION

At last! It's official! After 'falling into' each other's lives, and rapidly falling in love, the world's most photographed young couple have named the day.[1] Yes, His Royal Highness Prince Henry Charles Albert David of Wales and Ms Rachel Meghan Markle, of Toronto and Los Angeles, are going to get married.

1. Saturday 19th May 2018

The news is welcome, but comes as no surprise. And there are surely many more important events happening worldwide. Nevertheless, if Prince Harry's brother's wedding is anything to go by, he and Meghan can confidently expect a global TV audience of 2 billion or more to watch them exchange vows.

Why?

Why – apart from our natural pleasure at seeing people who seem happy, and apart from our sentimental excitement at the start of any new romantic enterprise – do we care?

No fairytale

Mercifully, the very silly word 'fairytale' is not being bandied about to describe Prince Harry's forthcoming marriage – unlike the wedding of his father and mother in 1981. However, as at any wedding, all who join in – if only by watching the celebrations on television – will probably want to wish that the new couple lives 'happily ever after'.

Hello strangers

Attending a wedding is a sign of closeness, friendship, family belonging. But most of us will never meet this year's princely bride and groom – or any royals, anywhere – and we certainly won't get to know them as friends.

Some of us may not believe in monarchy, or in the institution of marriage. We may not follow the Christian faith (any wedding held in a church is, after all, a solemn religious occasion). We may even feel outraged by public displays of inherited wealth, power and privilege, and consider formal, uniformed pomp and circumstance a ridiculous anachronism in the egalitarian 21st century. We may find lavish spending on flowers, frocks, food, drink and general flummery distasteful in a time of recession.

Love ~ and marriage?

Love seldom falls out of fashion, but getting married has become steadily less popular over the last hundred years or so.

in the early 21st century, statisticians tell us that only 22.8 single men out of every 1,000 are likely to marry in any one year, and 20.5 single women. When similar statistics were first calculated, in the 1860s, the equivalent figures were 58.7 per 1,000 for men and 50 per 1,000 for women.

So why all the fuss when a royal wedding is announced? Why the miles of print and acres of pictures? Why the hints and denials, the deferential interviews, the guesses and gossip? Why the souvenirs – tacky or tasteful? Why the flood of commentary, from the patriotic to the prurient? And why books like this?

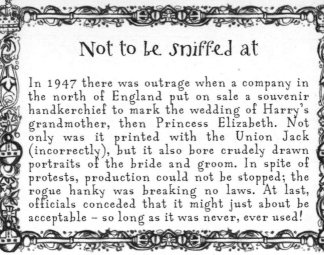

Not to be sniffed at

In 1947 there was outrage when a company in the north of England put on sale a souvenir handkerchief to mark the wedding of Harry's grandmother, then Princess Elizabeth. Not only was it printed with the Union Jack (incorrectly), but it also bore crudely drawn portraits of the bride and groom. In spite of protests, production could not be stopped; the rogue hanky was breaking no laws. At last, officials conceded that it might just about be acceptable – so long as it was never, ever used!

Is our enthusiasm for all things royal because

'the CROWN
...is something set above
The jangle and the jargon and the hate...'?

Poet Laureate John Masefield,
'On the Coming Marriage'

Surely not! Few people would agree with those words from 1947 today. If the British monarchy did not exist, we'd probably have to invent it, or else go to the trouble of choosing a president to be short-term head of state instead. And, as recent events reveal, that's not for the faint-hearted.

A reflection of ourselves?

It has been said that 'monarchy…is about magic'.[2] Perhaps. It is rather more likely that monarchy is a mirror reflecting our tastes and values back to us – but in an extremely selective way.

Over the centuries, royal families have changed, along with the societies they've been rooted in. And so today, in an age of obsession with cash, consumer brands and celebrity, the royals are the ultimate famous family, at least in the UK. We build them up to reflect our dreams and fantasies. We knock them down, projecting onto them, as individuals, our collective disappointments and fears.[3]

2. Daily Telegraph, *18 November 2010.*
3. *It's perhaps only fair to add that the royal mirror also reflects several rather more positive social concerns, such as heritage and conservation.*

Public appetite

Eagerly, oh so eagerly, we devour real or manufactured news about royal families. We cannot see too many photos of royal clothes, houses, parties, jewels and holidays, or listen to too much royal gossip – preferably about royal wrongdoings and/or royal love lives. (If the two are combined, it's a great way of selling books and newspapers.)

'Once the [royal] brides were English and pretty, the floodgates of schmalz opened.'

Historian David Starkey in the Daily Mail, *21 November 2010*

Why do we need to do this? Because we admire real-life royal people and their carefully created images? Because looking at wealth and privilege allows us to escape from harsh reality in tough economic times? Because the royals are ambassadors for (yes) or symbols of (surely not!) our nation? Or simply because young, attractive couples like Prince Harry and his fiancée are jolly good free entertainment, to amuse or distract us whatever the cost to their own personal privacy and peace of mind?

Sad to say, even royal sufferings fascinate us. We gloat, as well as sympathise, when the inhabitants of our national royal zoo sometimes feel the need to rattle the bars of their gilded cages. As Prince Harry's mother so tragically discovered, adoring attention from the public and the mass media is a deadly two-edged sword.

Them and us

Over 100 years ago, Victorian history-writer Walter Bagehot declared that 'A princely marriage is a brilliant edition of a universal fact.' But even though, for the past half-century, the British royal 'firm'[4] has been keen to portray itself as the embodiment of comfortable, conservative, upper-middle-class family values, royal lives are not – and cannot be – just like ours.

4. *This is the royal family's own nickname for itself, reportedly coined by Prince Philip.*

An awful wedding warning

"I know that I'm in love with this girl and I hope that she's in love with me. But we still had to sit down on the sofa and have some pretty frank conversations with her to say, 'What you're letting yourself in for, it's a big deal. It's not easy for anybody.' I know that at the end of the day, she chooses me, and I choose her. And therefore, whatever we have to tackle together, or individually, it'll always be us together as a team."

Prince Harry, BBC TV interview with Mishal Husain, 27th November 2017

Nor can royal weddings be like ours. As only fifth – soon to be sixth[5] – in line to the throne, Harry knows that his marriage will be public and political, however private and personal his feelings may be.

We all want to look nice in our own wedding photos, but the whole world will be scrutinising Harry's formal, fancy uniform and his bride's dress, hair, veil, bouquet and jewels – to say nothing of their choice of best man, bridesmaids and other attendants. The guest list will be picked over by pundits and social media vultures: too many celebs for dignity, or not enough for glamour? How simple, in contrast, if all we have to worry about is whether to invite Great Aunt Ethel, or how to keep drunken Uncle Fred away from prim Cousin Mabel.

5. Harry will be moved down one place in the royal line of succession to the throne once Prince William's third child is born in spring 2018.

And, although the words 'tradition' and 'history' almost always appear alongside any mention of grand royal events, royal weddings have varied quite alarmingly over the centuries. Royal chroniclers have recorded secret midnight ceremonies, scandalous elopements, bloodstained political dramas, sordid business deals, at least one kidnapping, some brisk, dutiful working honeymoons – and a few, just a few, real-life royal romances. Read on and find out more…

What's in a name?

Today, almost without thinking, we call monarchs 'king' or 'queen', and the younger members of royal families 'prince' or 'princess'. Technically, this is not always accurate. For example, Zara Phillips has no royal title, even though Queen Elizabeth II is her grandmother.

In the past, titles of ruling royalty ranged from mighty emperor to lowly count and countess. Their children might have the same titles, or be known simply as 'Lord' and 'Lady'. In this book we have – we hope – called past royal persons by their correct titles. We have, however, sometimes used the general terms 'prince' and 'princess' when referring to royalty, or for individuals to avoid confusion.

Q. *What was the 'Wedding of the Century' – over five hundred years ago?*

A. The marriage of Duke Charles the Bold of Burgundy and Margaret, sister of King Edward IV of England, in 1468. Celebrations, at Bruges in present-day Belgium, began with a 'Joyous Entry' for the bride: wearing a jewelled coronet, she was carried into the city on a golden litter pulled by white horses. Music filled the streets, which were hung with tapestries; the canals were lit by flaming torches, and the bridges were decked with flowers. Statues and royal coats of arms hung from the trees, and there was free wine for everyone. Later, there were plays, dances, tournaments and parades – and, of course, a splendid feast.

Q. Whose royal wedding went with a bang?

A. In 1886, French princess Amelia of Orleans wed the duke of Braganza in Portugal. The very moment the couple exchanged their vows in Lisbon cathedral, church bells rang, cannons boomed, and rockets screeched into the sky. At the same time, the sailors on board all Portuguese government ships in Lisbon harbour were ordered to kneel down and pray.

Q. Whose wedding shoes started a new fashion?

A. Princess Frederica of Prussia was petite and pretty, with very small hands and feet. The tiny jewelled slippers she wore at her wedding to the royal duke of York in 1791 were admired and copied. The fascinated prince ordered six pairs for his bride-to-be.

‘ We have to be clear
that there is nothing wrong
with arranged marriages.
If it's good enough for the
Royal Family, then people
shouldn't have a problem
with it... ’

Khalid Mahmood, MP for
Birmingham Perry Barr, 2001
(Birmingham Evening Mail)

CHAPTER ONE

A MARRIAGE HAS BEEN ARRANGED...

It would be murder! It would break every law known to man – and to God! And it would cause a right royal scandal! But Duke Ernst of Bavaria-Munich was not a man to shirk his duty. He knew what he must do, as a ruler and as a father. In 1435 he summoned his most trusted servants and issued secret orders: the girl must go!

What girl? And why? Her name was Agnes Bernauer, and she was a baker's daughter. No harm in that, surely? But Agnes, who was young and pretty, also worked as a maid in a Munich city bathhouse. She probably carried jugs of boiling water or flagons of wine to rich male customers as they enjoyed a relaxing hour or two, soaking in huge wooden tubs surrounded by cosy, private curtains. If Agnes had a few sips of a customer's wine, and if she lingered a while to (ahem) keep him company – well, Agnes's customers were certainly not complaining.

No-one else bothered much, either, until Duke Ernst heard that his son and heir Albert had been visiting Agnes's bathhouse. Before long, it was clear that the two had become close friends. It was even rumoured that they had held a secret wedding ceremony and were now man and wife.[1]

1. *They had, probably in 1432.*

Oh no!

Duke Ernst was horrified. This was absolutely *not* how royalty was meant to behave! Young Albert knew very well[2] that royal (and noble) marriages were arranged by parents for their children. Other close relatives, top churchmen, senior diplomats and leading politicians were also expected to offer suggestions and advice. Delicate marriage negotiations might take months or years; the wrong decision could have serious consequences – political, religious, dynastic…

2. *Possibly better than most. As a young child his parents had arranged for him to marry the daughter of a German nobleman. But before the wedding, she had run away with a handsome young page at her father's court. Another royal scandal!*

Multi-purpose

One day, young Albert would rule Bavaria-Munich.[3] To Duke Ernst and his advisors, the young man's marriage was therefore a matter of national concern. Albert's bride must be chosen to help his homeland, by expanding its frontiers, adding to its treasures, defending its religion, enhancing its prestige, winning strong new allies, ending a war, confirming a treaty – or, if possible, all these at the same time! Ideally, she should strengthen the fame, power, riches and glory of the ruling royal family, as well.

Young Agnes obviously could not fulfil any of these royal bridal functions. Instead, Duke Ernst thought, she would bring shame and ridicule to her husband, his family and the lands they ruled. No-one would respect a former servant; her children would never be allowed to rule. It would mean the end of Ernst's royal family – and maybe an end to his duchy, as well.

3. He did, as Duke Albert III the Pious, from 1438 to 1460.

Desperate measures

Carefully, Ernst made plans. He knew that young Albert's other great passions were fighting and hunting. (And he approved: both were very suitable skills for a strong, manly medieval ruler.) So he arranged a magnificent tournament – or else a splendid hunt (reports do not agree) – for Albert and his young noble friends to enjoy. While they were out of the way, poor Agnes was kidnapped and put on trial – for witchcraft. She was found guilty and drowned in the River Danube.

Later, Duke Ernst admitted that what he had done was wrong. He paid for a fine church to be built over Agnes's tomb, to show that he was sorry. But he had got his way: a most unsuitable marriage was over. After fleeing Bavaria, then returning to fight his father, young Albert made peace with his family. In 1437 he obeyed their wishes and married a rich, respectable, well-connected princess from a powerful state in north Germany.

Wedding winnings

No-one today could possibly approve of Duke Ernst's drastic action, but many people in the past would have sympathised with his feelings when he learned of his son's secret wedding. Marriage was first and foremost a matter of politics, statecraft, business, property, convenience, protection or sheer survival. It could also be royally profitable:

Catherine de' Medici (1519–1589), daughter of the duke of Urbino in Italy, was small, stout, studious, suspiciously fond of weird herbal medicines, and not very pretty. But her dowry (see page 43) included five cities, a large sum of money, and the promise of close political links with powerful Italian rulers, including the Pope. So, in 1553, she was married to the son (soon to be the heir) of the king of France.

In 1515, widowed **Princess Mary Rose Tudor** (sister of King Henry VIII of England) made a second marriage, to an English nobleman. Chroniclers debated: Was this wise? Would Mary have done more for her country if she'd married a foreign prince? Eventually they decided, and the answer was 'no'. By staying in England, Mary enriched the nation with the generous dower[4] (see page 43) she'd gained when her first husband died. The fact that she loved her second husband was irrelevant.

Religious rules

However, marriage was not just a practical arrangement. It was a sacrament – part of a holy way of living decreed by God. And Christian marriage was regulated by the Church, not by kings or governments.

According to Church law, a valid marriage happened when two people old enough to consent (12 for girls, 14 for boys, until 1875) agreed to take each other as husband and wife. Ideally, they did this in church, in front of witnesses. It was even better if they consummated the marriage by sleeping together soon afterwards. But, from around AD 110, none of these options was strictly necessary. It was the promise 'I take thee as

4. *10,000 silver marks per year – approaching £2 million today.*

my husband (or wife)' that made a marriage. If Duke Ernst's son and young Agnes had exchanged these words, in public or in private, they were legally married.

Church law also decreed that a marriage only ended when one of the partners died. Divorce was impossible: 'Whom God hath joined, let no man put asunder.' Kings and nobles could, and did, pay for clever lawyers to argue in Church law courts that an undesirable marriage had never been valid, but the process was expensive, long-winded and desperately uncertain. For high-ranking families like Duke Ernst's, the Pope in Rome was the final arbiter.[5] And his decisions were likely to be influenced by politics and family loyalties.

5. From the mid-16th century, in Protestant countries, other Church leaders replaced the Pope. But Christian rules about marriage remained much the same until the 19th century. Marriage outside the Church was legally possible, but socially and politically unacceptable for royal families. After all, most claimed that God had given them the right to rule!

Really, truly married?

According to Church law, there were only four reasons why a marriage could be annulled (declared non-valid):

1. Consanguinity
Close relatives (specifically, people sharing a great-great-great-grandmother) were not allowed to wed. Brothers or sisters were not permitted to marry their dead siblings' spouses, or widowed parents to marry their dead children's marriage partners.

Since most European royal families were related to each other, royal brides and grooms often obtained the Pope's permission to ignore these rules when they wanted to marry. But if they wanted to end the marriage, they could sometimes – many years later – persuade the Pope to revoke (cancel) his earlier permission.

This tactic was most famously tried by England's **King Henry VIII** at the start of his multiple-marriage saga (see pages 109–113). In 1509 he had married his brother's widow, Catherine of Aragon. But she had no male children, and by around 1525 he was in love with a new sweetheart. However, for fear of angering Catherine's nephew, Emperor Charles V – who had a *very* big army – the Pope declined to help Henry.

2. Pre-contract

If there was the slightest suspicion that a bride or groom had previously married another person using the words 'I take thee...', then any later marriage would not be valid while the original partners was still alive – even if the couple had never lived together as man and wife. Pre-contract could be very difficult to prove or disprove, as witnesses to the promise were not necessary.

King Edward IV of England (ruled 1461–1470 and 1471–1483) was famous for his roving eye and for his many, many mistresses. In 1464 he met a pretty widow, Elizabeth Woodville, while he was out hunting. Holding a fearsome knife to her throat, he demanded that she become his latest lover. But she refused, and insisted that they got married first. In secret, they exchanged the all-important promise 'I take thee...' – under an ancient oak tree, or so the traditional story says.

When news of the wedding leaked out – several months later, while Edward's advisors were planning a 'proper' wedding for him – the royal family and courtiers were disgusted and dismayed. Elizabeth came from such a low-ranking family! But the marriage could not be unmade.

3. Force

Both bride and groom were meant to give free consent to a marriage. But either could be bullied or bribed, and might be too terrified to protest. And if the couple had had sex – even if the bride was unwilling – then the marriage was valid.

Around 1047, Duke William of Normandy (better known today as **William the Conqueror**) sent a proposal of marriage to Matilda, daughter of the king of France. But William had been born out of wedlock, and Matilda haughtily refused him, saying she 'would marry no bastard'. William leapt on his horse, rode to the royal palace, stormed his way into Matilda's bedchamber, and dragged her round the room by her hair. Rather surprisingly, this savage courtship won Matilda's heart, and they enjoyed a long and happy marriage together.

4. Impotence,

or a complete refusal to have sex, made a marriage invalid, unless both husband and wife chose this chaste way of life together.

Saintly **King Edward the Confessor** of England (ruled 1042–1066) and his wife Edith had a sex-free marriage. Their religious devotion was admired (being a virgin was very holy), but their failure to produce a son to rule after them led to big political problems.

As always...

Duke Ernst would not have known this, but, in trying to control who his child married, he was following an extremely ancient tradition.

Almost three thousand years earlier, **Pharaoh Amenhotep III** of Egypt (ruled c.1390–c.1350 B.C.) wrote a letter full of scorn when the king of Babylon dared to ask for one of his daughters as a bride: 'Never since the beginning of time has the daughter of the king of Egypt been given in marriage to anyone.'[6] No foreigner – even a king – could possibly be good enough to marry a princess from Amenhotep's mighty Egypt.

The pharaohs were, however, happy to add hundreds of foreign princesses to their own royal harems. By arranging marriages with less powerful ruling families, they gained influence over smaller, weaker states, and grew rich from the dowries (sheep, cattle and slaves, laboriously trekked across the desert) that their new wives brought with them.

6. T Bryce, Letters of the Great Kings of the Ancient Near East, 2003.

Don't do it!

Royal families might also try to *prevent* marriages for political or financial reasons.

For example, in 1472, royal brothers **Prince Richard[7] and Prince Edward** of England quarrelled over a very rich heiress, Anne Neville. Edward hid Anne in a noble friend's house, disguised as a scullery maid. But Richard tracked her down, helped her seek sanctuary in a church, then married her – and got all her lands.

Centuries later, in 1719, **Princess Maria Clementina Sobieska** of Poland, on her way to marry Scottish prince James Edward Stuart, was kidnapped, probably by supporters of King George I of the United Kingdom. (Prince James was plotting against him.) The princess was locked up in a fortress under the watchful eyes of nuns, but her friends bribed the guards and she escaped. She married Prince James the following year.

7. *later King Richard III.*

Lucky Austria wins the wedding lottery!

Just over the frontier from Bavaria, and only a few years after Duke Ernst died (in 1438), the Hapsburg dynasty of Austria made such clever use of arranged marriages that poems were written about them. One line in particular became very famous:

'Bella gerant alii, tu felix Austria nube.'[8]

Less poetically speaking, it's fair to say that the Austrian royals were also extraordinarily lucky:

1470

Emperor Frederick III is head of the Hapsburg family in Austria, and things are looking pretty bad. He's lost control of Switzerland; he's shaken by civil wars. From the east, Hungarians are attacking (and they will conquer Austria in 1480).

1473

Don't despair, Frederick! Make plans to win money and power! How? By arranging marriages, of course. Duke Charles the Bold rules Burgundy, the richest, most glamorous and go-ahead small state in Europe. He has no sons – but he does have a daughter. Get to know them both.

8. *Let others make war; you, fortunate Austria, marry.*

1477

Duke Charles dies. Frederick quickly marries his son Maximilian to Charles's daughter Mary. Now the Hapsburgs control her lands.

1482

Mary dies, having produced a son, Philip. This lucky lad, Frederick's grandson, becomes duke of Burgundy; he's also heir to Frederick's (Hungarian-occupied) Austrian lands.

1490

Austria's conqueror, the king of Hungary,[9] dies suddenly, without children. Frederick grabs his chance and wins back Austria. Now his grandson Philip has an empire to inherit!

1496

Frederick died in 1493 but Maximilian now marries Philip, his son (Frederick's grandson), to Juana, the king of Spain's daughter.

1498

Max hopes that Spain will help fight Austria's enemy, France. But Juana will also be the next queen of Spain, once her father dies. What an enticing prospect!

1500

Philip and Juana have a son, Charles. He's a great-grandson to Frederick, and an heir for the Hapsburg family.

9. *Poor King Matthias Corvinus of Hungary had very bad luck in family matters. He married three times, and was first widowed at the age of only 12. All his wives died and left no sons to rule after him.*

1506
Philip dies, and Juana is very ill. Their son Charles is still a child, but one day he'll rule Spain and its fast-growing overseas empire.

1515
Maximilian marries his younger son to the daughter of the new king of Hungary. Now Austria's safe from Hungarian attack.

1516
Back in Spain, Juana's father dies. She's now queen, but still ill. (Cruelly, they call her 'Juana the Mad'.) Her son Charles, Frederick's great-grandson, becomes the new Spanish ruler.

1519
Maximilian dies, and Charles (yes, Frederick's great-grandson) inherits Burgundy and Austria, which he rules alongside Spain. He also inherits Frederick's title of Holy Roman Emperor – so he's the highest-ranking monarch in Europe.

1526
The new king of Hungary dies fighting the Turks. He has no sons, so his daughter becomes queen. Her husband (Maximilian's younger son, Frederick's grandson) takes over her kingdom. Lucky man! Lucky Austria! The Hapsburg family lands now stretch from Belgium to the borders of Turkey, and include a vast territory in the Americas. It's the largest western empire since ancient Roman times – and it's been won, in barely 50 years, mostly by arranged marriages.

Q. *Who took his mistress to his royal wedding?*

A. Prince John of Gaunt, fourth son of King Edward III of England. Keen to win a kingdom of his own, he arranged a marriage with Queen Constance of Castile in 1371. John's long-time mistress, Katherine Swynford, and their children travelled with him to Spain and appeared lovingly by John's side, even in front of his bride.

Q. *Which queen arranged her own marriage, then helped to murder her husband?*

A. Mary, Queen of Scots, in 1565. She fell in love with her cousin, the tall, dark, handsome, well-connected – but vicious and traitorous – Henry Darnley. Two years later, his house was blown up – and he was found strangled close by. Did Mary know about the plot to kill him? It's quite possible.

**‘ Ask for anything
you want – even
half my kingdom! ’**

*Celtic king Vortigern (mid-5th century AD)
to Saxon invader Hengist, asking to wed
Hengist's beautiful daughter. After the
marriage, Hengist took over Vortigern's
lands – as he had planned all along.*

**‘ In any country, a king
marrying a subject is looked
on as dishonourable. ’**

Britain's King George III, 1772

CHAPTER TWO

FAMILY AFFAIRS

In 1269, King John of Scotland wrote to his closest political ally, Philip IV, king of France, to say that he had recently sent:

'attorneys, procurators and special envoys...
to contract a betrothal and marriage between
Edward, our firstborn son and, what is more,
future heir, *and any female descendant or
kinswoman* of the said lord king...'[1]

1. Records of the Parliaments of Scotland, cited from: http://www.rps. ac.uk/search.php?a=fcf&fn=john_balliol_trans&id=id121&t=trans; our emphasis.

Yes indeed, King John wanted a wife for his son and heir. And he wanted that wife to come from the French royal family. Other than that, it didn't really matter *which* royal female sailed from France to Scotland to marry young Prince Edward; what was important was that the blood of kings and queens flowed in her veins.

Royal pick and mix

In 928, **King Æthelstan** of England sent two of his daughters on a long journey across Europe to the court of Emperor Henry I. His purpose? The emperor had agreed to choose one of them as a bride for his son Otto, and to pass the 'reject' on to be a wife for a less important prince in Burgundy.

Money matters

Along with his letter, King John sent a team of diplomats to France. It comprised two bishops and two knights (arranging royal marriages was an exercise in strategy, like chess). Their task was to negotiate:

- the royal bride's *dowry* – the land or money she would bring to her husband's family

- her *jointure* – land or goods to fund her widow's pension

- her *dower* or morning gift. In Anglo-Saxon times this had been handed to a bride on the morning after her wedding night as a sign of the bridegroom's approval(!), but it later became a way of providing royal wives with an income to pay for clothes and entertainments.

King John's team also had to finalise all the other details of the royal marriage settlement (that is, contract). This covered everything from the bride's religious beliefs and future political alliances to the castles and jewellery she might hope to enjoy or the number of foreign ladies' maids (from her home country) that she could have living with her.

Marriage menace?

In 1290, 7-year-old Princess Margaret, the **'Maid of Norway'** and heir to the Scottish crown, set sail from Scandinavia to Orkney to claim her inheritance. According to a treaty agreed with Scotland's much stronger neighbour, England,[2] Margaret would become Scotland's queen, then marry the future king Edward II of England.

Had this marriage happened, England would have taken over the smaller, weaker Scottish kingdom. But poor little Margaret died on the voyage, and Scotland stayed independent for the next 300 years.

Bridal bonus

In 1469 a marriage was arranged between **King James III of Scotland** and Princess Margaret of Denmark. The wedding went ahead – but Margaret's father could not afford to pay her agreed dowry. So King James seized Orkney and the Shetland Isles instead; for around 600 years they had been ruled by Denmark, but now they became part of Scotland.

2. *Scotland was hardly in a position to refuse.*

Give and take

Over in France, King Philip proved willing. He agreed to a marriage between King John's son and a French royal lady; he suggested Jeanne, daughter of his younger brother Charles. He offered a rich dowry (25,000 *livres tournois*)[3] and demanded a handsome dower (£1,500 sterling[4] for Jeanne, every year).

But King Philip also made it clear that the wedding would only take place on certain conditions. King John must help France fight against England and send his troops south on raids across the border. In return, France would help the Scots fight against the English.

• Cautious? Yes!

• Prudent? Yes!

• Statesmanlike? Yes!

• Warlike? Yes!

• But romantic? No, no, no!

3. *worth around £75,000 today.*
4. *worth around £800,000 today.*

The 'Grandmother of Europe'

Many hundreds of years later, Britain's remarkable **Queen Victoria** (ruled 1837–1901) was still continuing a very similar marriage tradition. By encouraging her nine children to wed other European royalty,[5] Victoria created a vast extended royal family – and a new nickname for herself.

Victoria's children

1. **Victoria** (1840–1901), m. German Emperor Frederick III

2. **Edward** (1841–1910), m. Princess Alexandra of Denmark

3. **Alice** (1843–1878), m. Grand Duke Ludwig IV of Hesse

4. **Alfred** (1844–1900), m. Grand Duchess Marie Alexandrovna of Russia

5. **Helena** (1846–1923), m. Prince Christian of Schleswig-Holstein

6. **Louise** (1848–1939), m. the future 9th Duke of Argyll

5. *The Queen did not object to love matches – after all, she had adored her own husband. But love ideally happened in the right way, in the right place, at the right time…*

7. **Arthur** (1850–1942), m. Princess Louise Margaret of Prussia

8. **Leopold** (1853–1884), m. Princess Helena of Waldeck-Pyrmont

9. **Beatrice** (1857–1944), m. Prince Henry of Battenburg

How common!

Only one of Queen Victoria's children married a member of a non-royal family. And she wed the heir to a dukedom – the highest possible rank of British nobility, just one degree lower than royalty. By the late 19th century, that was – just about – acceptable. But traditionally, if royalty dared to wed one of their less high-ranking subjects – known as 'commoners'[6] – the marriage was either condemned as 'impolitic and unprecedented'[7] or it led to scandal. It might even be against the law.

6. *The term is generally taken to mean anyone who is not a member of a royal family.*
7. *Tudor chronicler Polydore Vergil (c.1470–1555), describing Edward IV's secret marriage (see page 32).*

Ranks and titles (UK)

Title	Form of address	Rank
King/Queen	Your Majesty	ROYALTY
Prince/Princess	Your Royal Highness	
Duke/Duchess[8]	Your Royal Highness	
Duke/Duchess	Your Grace	HEREDITARY PEERAGE[9]
Marquess	Your Lordship	
Marchioness	Your Ladyship	
Earl	Your Lordship	
Countess	Your Ladyship	
Viscount	Your Lordship	
Viscountess	Your Ladyship	
Baron	Your Lordship	
Lady	Your Ladyship	
Baronet	Sir	
Lady	Lady	
Knight	Sir	KNIGHT-HOOD[10]
Lady	Lady	
Dame	Dame	

8. Some dukes are of royal rank, e.g. Prince Philip, duke of Edinburgh.
But royal dukes' wives are not automatically entitled to be called 'Royal
Highness'. For example, when the Prince of Wales married Mrs Wallis
Simpson (see pages 94–95), King George VI refused permission.
9. There are also life peers (usually barons and baronesses), who hold
their rank and title for their lifetime only and cannot pass on either
to their descendants.
10. Knights and dames cannot pass their rank or title to their
descendants, either.

Almost worthy...

In 1660, **Prince James** (brother of King Charles II and later to be King James II) was secretly married – around midnight, in a friend's quiet, private house – to Mistress[11] Anne Hyde. Like today's Catherine Middleton, Anne was a commoner – though Little Miss Average she was *not*. Her father was a senior royal official, and she herself was 'maid-in-waiting' (confidential assistant) to the Princess Royal. Anne was not pretty, but she was lively, intelligent, strong-minded, sensible and very well-informed. She was admired by many in royal circles, including the French ambassador. But even his warm praise had a sting in its tail: Anne had 'courage, cleverness, and energy *almost* worthy of a king's blood' (our emphasis).

To the horror of many English people, Anne was also a Roman Catholic. And, shamefully for the royal dignity, they mocked her ample figure in highly offensive terms. Anne's own father was scandalised – and feared for his

11. *Mistress: a term of respect for an adult woman, married or not; similar to French* Madame.

49

career. Aware that his daughter had insulted the monarchy by marrying without proper permission, he advised King Charles (now Anne's royal brother-in-law) to send her to the Tower of London and cut off her head!

...to be the mother of queens!

Prince James was famously brave, silly – and unfaithful. But, in his own way, he was devoted to Anne, and so he stood by her. After news of their secret marriage leaked out, he wedded her again, publicly. And – in spite of Anne's early death (aged 33, in 1671) and her 'commoner' blood – two of their children became queens of England: Mary II (born 1662, reigned 1689–1694) and Anne (born 1665, reigned 1702–1714).

No papists!

After **Prince James** himself became Catholic following the death of his wife, British royalty was banned from marrying any member of the Church of Rome. That law[12] remained in force until 2015. So, in 2006, the son of the UK's royal duke of Kent had to get special permission from Queen Elizabeth II to marry his Roman Catholic bride – not secretly in this case, but very publicly, in the Pope's own palace-city, the Vatican.

In 2010 a House of Commons committee declared that banning British royals from marrying Catholics was against the Human Rights Convention. Parliament passed a new Succession to the Crown Act in 2013; it became law two years later.

Royal enough for you?

In 1923, when the crown prince of Sweden (the future **King Gustav Adolf**) proposed to **Lady Louise Mountbatten**, the Swedish prime minister had to telephone his British counterpart to check that the bride-to-be was 'properly' royal. Commoner marriages were illegal for Swedish royals. He was informed that Lady Louise was a great-granddaughter of Queen Victoria. What more could anyone want?

12. the Act of Settlement, 1701.

51

Bad habits!

It took another royal scandal (or two, or three…) before marriage to non-royalty became illegal for British princes and princesses, without the Sovereign's express permission.

The Royal Marriages Act of 1772 was passed on the orders of King George III, who was furious when his brother **Prince Henry** married Mrs Anne Horton, a widowed – but very flirtatious – nobleman's daughter, after meeting her at the fashionable and rather racy new resort of Brighthelmstone.[13] It was also said – though never proved – that Henry had previously wed another commoner, Olive Wilmot, but had deserted her after she gave birth to their child.

King George claimed that such democratic 'measures' (as he called these unsuitable romances) would increase the royal family's (already considerable) unpopularity, and maybe even lead to civil war. Prince Henry and his wife fled overseas.

13. *now known as Brighton.*

George became even angrier when another brother, **Prince William**, admitted that he, too, had secretly married – six years previously! His wife was the illegitimate daughter of a noble, but not royal, family; now she was pregnant. What should they do? King George's reply to the pair was brief and to the point: go away from the royal court, and stay away!

That was that, or so King George must have thought. With the new law safely passed, there should be no more unsuitable royal weddings. But then, in 1785, his oldest son and heir, **Prince George**, chose a doubly illegal bride. She was Mrs Maria Fitzherbert, a commoner and a Catholic. She was also a widow, twice over.

Maria would not be satisfied with being the Prince's lover – she demanded marriage, or nothing. Prince George was infatuated; he wrote her 30-page love letters, suggested that they run away together to America, and, when she rejected his advances, tried to commit suicide. At last, Prince George agreed to a secret wedding ceremony. But because it took place after 1772, the marriage was illegal. Whatever the prince and Maria may have believed, their marriage never existed in law.

👑 And nor did Royal Secret Wedding Number 4. (Poor old King George must have wondered what on earth he could do to stop them; an Act of Parliament ought to have been enough!) This time, in 1793, his sixth son **Augustus** secretly married Lady Augusta Murray. Not valid!

In spite of his grand passion, Prince George soon tired of Maria Fitzherbert and began chasing new mistresses. In 1795 he was bribed by King George (who offered to pay off the Prince's alarming debts) to marry the very royal, though most unsavoury, Princess Caroline of Brunswick.

But that is another story…[14]

14. See pages 173–174.

Oh dear, what can the matter be?

Six royal princesses trapped in the nunnery...

No, they didn't actually sing that in 1790, but they might well have done. Sadder and wiser after so many secret weddings, King George III was determined not to let his six daughters rush into unsuitable marriages. Instead, they lived at home with their royal parents in Windsor Castle – where they were all extremely bored, lonely and unsatisfied. They themselves complained that it was like living in a nunnery.

1797: Princess Charlotte, 31, marries a German prince.

1810: Princess Amelia, 27, dies unmarried.

1816: Princess Mary, 40, marries a British royal duke.

1818: Princess Elizabeth, 48, marries a German duke.

1840: Princess Augusta, 71, dies unmarried.

1848: Princess Sophia, 70, dies unmarried.

Q: When is a royal marriage not a royal marriage?

A: When it's morganatic!

Morgan what? The name comes from *Morgen*, the German word for 'morning', and it shares the same origins as the rather humiliating tradition of the 'morning gift' described on page 43. But by around 1500, it was being used to describe a marriage between a royal or noble man and a low-ranking woman. They became legal man and wife, approved by Church and state, but the husband's rank, titles and wealth were not shared with or inherited by the wife or her children.

The custom of morganatic marriage did not exist in Britain (several kings might have found life easier if it had), but it was widespread in continental Europe. For example:

King Erik XIV of Sweden married his servant Karin Mansdotter twice – the first time morganatically, in 1567, the next time royally, in 1568.

In 1615, **King Christian IV** of Denmark married for the second time – morganatically and reluctantly. His bride was Kirsten Munk, a young Danish noblewoman. At first, King Christian had only

wanted to make Kirsten his mistress, but her mother persuaded him that anything less than marriage would be dishonourably unroyal. Kirsten had 12 children, but the king refused to believe that the youngest, a girl, was his. He accused Kirsten of witchcraft, as well as adultery, and locked her away in prison. Years later (in 1648), on his deathbed, the king summoned Kirsten to ask her forgiveness. But he died before she could reach him.

Empress Marie Louise, wife of French emperor Napoleon I, morganatically married an Italian noble, the count of Parma, after Napoleon died.

Prince Philip, duke of Edinburgh, is descended from ancestors who were married morganatically in 1851: German Prince Alexander of Hesse and Polish Countess Julia von Hauke.

Pity the poor parents!

Finding a suitable bride or groom – of whatever rank – for royal offspring often was not easy:

In 1926, the Dutch minister of Foreign Affairs was said to have drawn up a 'bridegroom checklist'. Why? To vet possible husbands for **Princess Juliana**, the daughter and heir of Queen Wilhelmina.

The young men ought to be:

- **royal** (from an old-established European ruling family)

- **Protestant**

- **healthy** (and especially not suffering from haemophilia, like so many of Queen Victoria's descendants)

- **wealthy** (so that it did not look as if the groom was marrying for money)

- **intelligent** (Juliana was clever and well educated)

- **of good reputation** (many young princes were disqualified for wild behaviour)

- **from a respectable family**, with no history of divorce

- *not* **German** – they were enemies of the Dutch just a few years before.

- and *not* **Dutch** – because Juliana outranked all her subjects.

The minister did not find the right man for the job. Juliana had to wait 11 long years until her story had a happy ending – and an unexpected one. In 1936, at the Winter Olympics in Bavaria, she herself met a most unlikely partner: a man not born a prince, with divorced parents, a history of health problems, a dangerous love of speedboats and fast cars, and a fondness for Paris nightlife and cocktails. Above all, he was a German, and (although only on paper) a member of the Nazi party.

Their royal marriage lasted for 66 years.

My husband and I...

Arranged or not, in the past the average royal marriage did not last very long. Kings or queens either died young, or quarrelled and separated. Britain's Queen Elizabeth II is the first ruling monarch to celebrate a platinum wedding anniversary. By 2017, she and her husband, Prince Philip, duke of Edinburgh, had been married for 70 years.

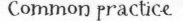

Common practice

By the end of the 20th century it was not unusual for members of royal families to marry commoners. All four of British Queen Elizabeth II's children did so – two of them twice. However, British royal traditions mean that 'commoner' husbands and wives are not given their own royal titles. Ms Markle will not become 'Princess Meghan' when she marries, just 'Princess Henry of Wales'.

Among other royal families, getting permission to wed a commoner has not always been easy. For example, King Harald V of Norway waited nine years to marry dressmaker Sonja Haraldson in 1968. He told his father, who opposed the wedding, that he would never marry anyone else. Since Harald was the sole heir to the crown, that would have meant the end of the Norwegian royal family!

Crown Princess Victoria of Sweden faced her father's anger[15] and public scorn by falling in love with country boy Daniel Westling, but married him triumphantly in 2010. Quipped Swedish author Stan Hedman: 'It was like a fairytale – she kissed her gym trainer and she got a prince.'

15. *though he later gave his consent.*

Q. Which ambitious mother and daughter both hoped to marry the same king?

A. In AD 956, when he should have been taking part in his solemn coronation ceremony, young Anglo-Saxon King Eadwig the All-Fair (aged 15) was found lounging on a couch with noble teenager Aelfgifu – and her mother. Both had hopes of marrying him. The young king was soundly thrashed by Abbot (later Saint) Dunstan, and dragged back to his royal duties.

Eadwig married Aelfgifu, but in 957 the archbishop of Canterbury made the pair separate, because they were too closely related according to Church laws.

Q. Whose family forbade the wedding?

A. Princess Margaret's, in 1955. The British princess fell in love with a dashing royal courtier, Group Captain Peter Townsend. But he was divorced, and that displeased the Queen Mother, the British government and the Church of England. As a compromise, it was suggested that Princess Margaret give up her royal rights, then marry and live overseas. The princess would not agree. In 1960 she wed the photographer Antony Armstrong-Jones (Lord Snowdon) instead; they divorced 18 years later.

❝ They have brought me a bat! ❞

Exclamation by King Charles II of England on first seeing his future bride, Catherine of Braganza, in 1662. Catherine was wearing extravagant Portuguese royal fashions: her wide dark cloak and stiffened skirts spread out on either side of her, like a bat's wings.

❝ I have been deceived! She is not beautiful. ❞

French King Henry IV, on meeting his future bride Marie de' Medici, 1600

CHAPTER THREE

STRANGERS IN THE NIGHT

✦

In 1736 a 17-year-old girl named Augusta arrived in London after an exhausting journey by horse-drawn carriage and sailing ship from northern Germany. It was the first time that she had ever been away from home, and she did not speak a word of English. (Her mother told her that now the British people had German kings – George I and II – they would be speaking German, too.) Sweet, gentle, timid, not very bright and pathetically eager to please, Augusta was also shaking with terror.

Augusta was hurried to the palace, dressed in a magnificent robe, and led to the altar. There she found Prince Frederick, heir to the throne of England; within a hour, she had stumbled her way through the wedding service (he shouted the words of the marriage vows into her ear; she repeated them, phonetically) and they were man and wife.

Still shaking, Augusta knelt before the king (George II) to receive the royal blessing – and then was very, very sick, all over the queen.

Dutiful daughters

Few royal brides were quite so traumatised by their wedding as poor Princess Augusta, but most of them, like her, had to marry strangers. How did they cope with the prospect? They managed, partly because they had been brought up with the knowledge that this was what the future held in store for them; and partly because they knew that there were not many other options.

Religious – or royal?

For royal daughters, the only real alternative to marriage was to become a nun.

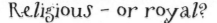 That was the choice of pious Italian **Princess Mary (or Maria) of Modena.** But Mary – unfortunately, from her point of view – was also rather beautiful, and caught the eye of an English envoy who visited her homeland. Her parents were delighted when he suggested a royal wedding, but Mary (aged 14) screamed and wept for two days and nights when told that she must marry widowed Prince James (the future King James II and VII), who was 25 years older than her.

A few weeks after the marriage (which was in 1673) Mary wrote to the head of the convent where she had hoped to spend her days: 'I cannot yet get used to this state of life ... So I weep a lot and mourn.'

Mary later became very fond of James. But this love was bittersweet. She wrote:

'It was sinful for any one to love an earthly creature as I loved him, but the fault brought its own punishment in the pain I suffered on discovering that I was not the exclusive object of his regard.'

Cited in M. Hopkirk, Queen Over the Water: Mary Beatrice of Modena, Queen of James II, *1953*

father knows best?

Few royal fathers shared King George III's wish to keep his daughters at home (see page 55), and even fewer were prepared to listen to a daughter who protested that she simply could not, would not, marry her intended bridegroom. No! Girls were useful national assets, to be married off to the most important husbands royal marriage-makers could find.

Princess Charlotte, daughter of the future King George IV and his queen Caroline, was a victim – and a problem. Throughout her childhood she was used, or ignored, by both her parents as a weapon in their continuous squabbles with one another.

Charlotte grew up fast, and by the time she was 15 was already provoking scandal. Her clothes were revealing! Her manners were free and easy! She was a minx! A tomboy!

Charlotte's father planned that she should marry Dutch Prince William (later King William II of the Netherlands). Reluctantly she agreed to meet; William was drunk, and she disliked him. But she did agree to sign the wedding contract, ready for a possible future marriage.

However, Charlotte had already fallen in love, several times, with her cousin and with his friends: dukes, princes and army officers. She held secret meetings with one Prussian prince, and tried to run away from home to be with him. After this, she told her father to destroy the contract she had signed: 'No arguments, no threats, will ever bend [my will] to marrying Prince William.'

At last, in 1816, Charlotte and her father agreed to compromise. She would marry a respectable prince serving in the Russian army, Leopold of Saxe-Coburg-Saalfeld. It was time to settle down – she was 20.

Just over a year later, Charlotte died in childbirth.

from the cradle

To prevent problems like Princess Charlotte, and to make the best use of their marriageable assets, royal families traditionally arranged marriages among very young children. So did rich nobles, who were often given the wardship (guardianship) of rich or royal orphans. They looked after the young heir or heiress until it was time to arrange a marriage; meanwhile, they pocketed all the income from their ward's lands, farms and castles.

In 1306 **King Edward I** of England began marriage negotiations with Burgundy when one of his daughters was only four days old. Sadly, she died aged 5, so the planned marriage never happened.

In 1396 **Princess Isabelle** of France, aged 6 or 7, married King Richard II of England. She was persuaded to agree to the match by being told that she 'would be a great lady'.

In 1937, the future **Queen Elizabeth II** of the United Kingdom was only 11 years old – and had not yet been told that she would one day reign as queen. But five possible future bridegrooms, from four foreign royal families, were already under discussion by courtiers:

- **Prince Charles of Luxembourg**, aged 9
- **Prince Gorm of Denmark**, aged 17
- **Prince Olaf of Denmark**, aged 13
- **Prince Philip of Greece**, aged 15
- **Prince Wilhelm Victor of Germany**, aged 17.

Q. Which prince wore a false beard and moustache – which slipped – to woo a possible bride?

A. The future King Charles I. In 1622, with his friend and helper the duke of Buckingham, he went to spy on the Spanish princess his father hoped he might marry. They dressed up in rather amateurish disguises, calling themselves Mr Smith and Mr Brown.

Past, present, future

Tiny children obviously could not marry in any meaningful way, but royal parents did their best to bind them together by betrothing (also called *espousing*) them.

Betrothal was similar to marriage, except that the couple exchanged promises in the future, rather than the present tense: 'I *will* take thee as my husband/wife.' These promises could be unmade at a later date, so long as the couple did not have sex together. Or they could be repeated in the present tense: 'I take thee...' some time in years to come, to make a permanent, valid marriage.

For political reasons, or simply to impress royal friends (and enemies), betrothals were staged with elaborate ceremonies, just like a wedding. Afterwards, betrothed princesses were often sent to live in their future husbands' royal castles. There they were taught the local language and and learned how to behave as a queen. Each different court had its own rigid rules of etiquette – and apparel, as King Charles II discovered so dramatically (see page 62).

But betrothals contained a hidden threat, as well as a marriage promise. The little princesses were not just pampered royal guests – but also hostages. If their old country quarrelled with their new homeland, their marriage might be called off. Then they'd be alone, without friends or money, in hostile territory. Who knew what might happen?

In 1100 **Matilda**, the daughter of Henry I of England, was sent, aged 8, to live with the family of her future husband, Holy Roman Emperor Henry V. She did wed him, but he died in 1125. She was sent back to England (surplus to requirements) as a widow, aged 22 – and was received as a hostile stranger! She had spent so long overseas that everyone thought she was German.

A few fortunate princesses were happy in their gilded royal 'prisons'. Clever, charming **Mary, Queen of Scots**, aged 6, was sent from war-torn Scotland to wealthy, luxurious, sophisticated France – and she loved it. She got to know, and feel sorry for, her strange betrothed husband (a weak, sickly, miserable prince who was to rule France briefly as Francis II) and was praised as 'the most perfect child' by her French royal father-in-law, Henry II.

'Big fish marks Japan's royal betrothal.' This striking headline in Australian paper *The Age* (21 March 2005) refers to the Japanese tradition of presenting beautiful sea bream (fish) at a formal betrothal ceremony. Why? Because the bream's Japanese name, *tai*, also means 'celebratory'. The happy bride-to-be was **Princess Nori**.

Marriage-makers

As we have seen, royal envoys were often sent to seek out royal brides or grooms and arrange their marriages. They also took part in proxy betrothals and even marriages, solemnly standing in for an absent or underage bride or groom, and speaking for them during the ceremony. Although this sometimes had a comic element (see page 75), theirs was a very responsible – and sometimes thankless – task. At least one ambassador paid with his life for suggesting the wrong bride.

Henry VIII engineered Thomas Cromwell's execution, allegedly for treason, after Cromwell had arranged his royal master's disastrous fourth marriage, to German Princess Anne of Cleves.

Rather than rely on a written description of his monarch's possible bride (the Tudors were very particular – see opposite), Cromwell despatched Henry's court painter, the brilliant Hans Holbein, to record the Princess's attractions in oils – twice.

Both pictures still survive, and show us a young woman, very richly dressed, looking with a calm, confident gaze right back at the viewer. Her face is pleasant – 'of middling beauty', according to the French ambassador at the time. What's more, Anne looks sensible and intelligent.

Henry VIII was delighted – until he met her! 'She is nothing so fair as she hath been reported', he complained, bitterly. He could not, or would not, consummate the marriage (see pages 112–113).

In every detail

In 1505, after his wife had died, **King Henry VII** of England sent ambassadors to Spain to report on a possible new bride. Pity the poor envoys! It was their task – without causing offence – to provide answers to 24 very detailed questions about the young lady's character and physique, set by the king. Somehow, they had to 'see her hands bare' (royalty often wore jewelled gloves) and 'note the fashion of them...thick or lean...long or short'. Encouragingly (or perhaps just diplomatically), the ambassadors reported that the candidate's hands were 'right faire'.

Proxies play the part

Pity also the special group of ambassadors sent, not to 'lie abroad for their country', as the famous diplomatic pun has it, but to take part in proxy wedding and betrothal ceremonies on behalf of their royal superiors, hundreds of miles away. Always men, they had to pretend to be the royal groom – or the bride! – pronounce the necessary vows before priests, and then – well, not exactly 'lie' with their new proxy husband or wife, but certainly take part in a public 'bedding' ceremony. This mock wedding night (which usually lasted only a few minutes, and was followed by a hearty feast) symbolised the consummation of the marriage by the real bride and groom, and made the match legally valid.

Why go through such a performance? Proxy weddings and betrothals were royal insurance policies, held as soon as possible after marriage negotiations were finalised. Their purpose? To make sure that neither side in an arranged marriage changed their mind and tried to get out of the deal. Very often there was a long time to wait before even the most eagerly arranged wedding could be held. The bride or groom might be too young, or – very often – might live hundreds of miles distant from one another.

In 1282 an English ambassador in Spain, Sir John de Vescy, had to pretend to be **Princess Eleanor**, daughter of

King Edward I of England, and go through a proxy marriage with **King Alfonso III** of Aragon. Sad to say, Princess Eleanor – although legally a married woman from the time of the proxy marriage onwards – never met her husband. The wedding date was delayed by his political quarrels with the Pope, and Alfonso died before his bride could make the journey to Spain.

Although proxy weddings were an extremely serious matter – as we have seen (pages 36–38), the fate of nations or empires could depend on the right choice of royal marriage partner – these events could have their funny side:

In 1514, after the marriage of Princess **Mary Rose Tudor** and **King Louis XII** of France had been agreed (see page 90–91), the French ambassador to the Tudor court took part in a proxy marriage – and bedding – in England. Together, he and Mary Rose were led to a splendid royal bed, where she lay down, fully clothed and decked in jewels. The ambassador remained clothed as well, except for one of his stockings. This he rolled down and removed, delicately and decorously. Then he lay down beside the princess, and gently let his bared leg touch one of her own royal limbs. In normal circumstances, such an act would be treason, and he'd have been executed. But, as part of a proxy marriage, it proved to the world that Mary Rose and King Louis were really, truly married.

Careless – and caring

However, for some royal bridegrooms, marrying a stranger – even a stupid one – did not seem to matter:

When **François, duke of Brittany**, met his future bride, Princess Isobel of Scotland, in 1442, he was 'more moved by her fair face than her womanly understanding', and claimed it was enough for her to 'know her husband in the dark from another man'.

In a very different way, clever, capable, musical[1] **Princess Anne of England** came to care for her unprepossessing husband, Dutch Prince William IV of Orange, whom she married in 1734. Anne's father, King George II, cruelly called William 'a baboon', and one of the court gossips rumoured that William's breath 'was more offensive than it is possible…to imagine'. But Anne found William kind (and very popular with ordinary people), and agreed with her father's more thoughtful courtiers that he was:

1. *She was Handel's favourite pupil and he wrote the music for her wedding.*

'perfectly well bred and civil... and with an ease and freedom that is seldom acquired but by a long knowledge of the world.'

But other royal husbands and wives were determined to find real love with partners they had chosen for themselves – or at least to enjoy the thrill of a clandestine love affair...

Q. Which royal bridegroom didn't meet his bride until months after the marriage?

A. King James VI of Scotland, in 1589. He was married in August by proxy to Princess Anne of Denmark; he was in Scotland, she was in Copenhagen. A few days later the new queen set sail, but her ship was nearly wrecked by furious storms[2] and sought shelter in Norway. James did not know what had happened until mid-October. Then, straight away, he set off to find her, despite the winter weather. They finally met in Oslo at the end of November – and began a month of celebrations.

2. *James blamed these on witchcraft.*

"I am born for the happiness
or misery of a great nation,
and consequently must often
act contrary to my passions."

British King George III, 1759

"I have found it impossible
to carry the heavy burden
of responsibility, and to
discharge my duties as
king as I would wish to do,
without the help and support
of the woman I love."

*King Edward VIII
(later duke of Windsor), 1936*

CHAPTER four

ALL YOU NEED IS LOVE?

K ings, queens, princes and princesses are all made of human flesh and blood. But almost everywhere, in every century, they have been required to put their royal duties before their own individual needs and feelings. Like King George III (quoted opposite), they have been expected to make personal sacrifices for the good of the nations they ruled.

In fact, **George III** was one of the lucky ones: he came to love his wife dearly. She was Princess Charlotte of Mecklenburg-Strelitz, whom he selected, without meeting, from a list of possible German brides, and married in 1761. Charlotte became his trusted friend and advisor, and nursed him devotedly during his long episodes of mental illness.

Hearts and minds

Admittedly, romantic love was not regarded as essential for many marriages in the past, among royalty or commoners. But, even so, living without mutual affection or respect must have been a strain for many royal couples. So how did they manage? Did they seek to repress all their feelings? Or did they look elsewhere for companionship, friendship, or even love?

Some royals, like Scots **King John** in his marriage negotiations with France (see pages 41–45), poured their passions into politics. In John's letters to the French king, he declared that he 'desired' the king's friendship 'with all our heart'. Today, we might expect words like 'desire' and 'heart' to be used by an eager young man wooing his chosen bride. But King John's letter did not even mention the thoughts or feelings of his eldest son or the unknown French princess who was to marry him. Their personal happiness (or otherwise) was not important.

How would King John, or his son, have reacted to the recent declaration by **Prince Harry** that he knew Meghan Markle was 'The One' 'the very first time we met'? Alas, we can never know. If only time travel were possible!

A good royal girl ~ but tragic

Some royals were simply obedient – and suffered heartache – like the teenage **Grand Duchess Alexandra Pavlovna** of Russia, described as the 'prettiest, sweetest and most innocent of the available princesses in Europe'. In 1796, as soon as Alix turned 13, her grandmother, Empress Catherine the Great, began to arrange her marriage; the chosen bridegroom was young King Gustav IV of Sweden. All went well – the young couple soon fell in love – until King Gustav started to read the marriage contract. It stated that his bride would remain a member of the Russian Orthodox Church, like the rest of her family. But Gustav and his Swedish subjects were Protestants! A queen who did not worship in their way was unacceptable.

Gustav rushed from the palace, where he was due to take part in a splendid betrothal ceremony, leaving little Alexandra ashamed and broken-hearted. The empress was so angry that she fell ill and died soon after.

Three years later, Alexandra's father, Tsar Paul I, arranged another marriage for her. This time, the wedding did take place; the groom was Archduke Joseph of Austria, Russia's ally against France. But Alexandra was not happy: her mother-in-law and the courtiers were jealous and disapproving. Barely a year after the wedding, dutiful Alexandra died in childbirth, aged just 17.

With friends like these...

Other kings and queens went looking for love – or passionate friendships – outside marriage, sometimes with unhappy consequences.

Queen Anne of England was devotedly attached to her childhood friend Sarah Churchill for over 30 years, and faced many (probably unjustified) accusations that the pair were lovers. They parted in 1710, after a jealous quarrel over Anne's new friendship with a younger lady-in-waiting.

More alarmingly, other royal ladies invested far too much trust – and far too many emotions – in friendships with dubious, but charming or charismatic, characters.

In Russia, **Empress Alexandra**'s links with faith-healer Grigori Rasputin caused a tremendous scandal until he was murdered in 1916. Alexandra was trying to find help for her haemophiliac son, but Rasputin's sordid, drunken private life and supposedly irresistible mystic powers cast suspicion on the whole royal family.

In the same way, over 100 years earlier in the 1770s and 1780s, French **Queen Marie Antoinette**'s dependence on very, very expensive designers, dressmakers, hairdressers and jewellers made the French royal family even more unpopular than it already was. Marie Antoinette spent lavishly on luxury goods, hoping that this 18th-century retail therapy might banish her feelings of inadequacy and isolation. She intended no harm, but at the time many French peasants were close to starvation. They demanded – and got – a revolution.

Q. *Which queen allowed herself to be kidnapped for love?*

A. Mary, Queen of Scots. Just a few weeks after her husband was murdered (in 1567; see page 39), she was carried off and raped by James Bothwell, an ambitious Scottish nobleman who claimed to love her. After that, she had to agree to marry him.

By royal command

Always, everywhere, extra-marital romance – or at least sex – was much easier for royal men. Although Church leaders disapproved, it was the accepted tradition for kings and princes to have mistresses.

Few, perhaps, went so far as French **King Louis XV** (ruled 1715–1774), who was rumoured to have set up what can only be called a private brothel, where all his junior mistresses could live together. (It was nicknamed the *Parc aux Cerfs* – literally the Deer Park, but if the story is true we might freely translate it as 'Happy Hunting Ground').

Kings who were loving and faithful to their wives, like **King Charles I** of England,[1] were so unusual as to cause comment – especially when Charles declared himself 'the happiest king in Christendom' after the birth of the couple's sixth child – and meant it.

---

1. *Well, certainly once his favourite the duke of Buckingham had died, three years after Charles's marriage. Charles I's queen, Princess Henrietta Maria of France, was an ideal partner for him: witty, elegant, gracious, tactful, and sharing his love of all the arts.*

'Too happy':
Victoria and Albert

Queen Victoria's marriage to her cousin, Prince Albert of Saxe-Coburg-Gotha, was not exactly arranged, but it was carefully planned. Their mutual uncle, King Leopold I of the Belgians, advised his brother, Albert's father, and his sister, Victoria's mother, on the upbringing and marriages of their children.

Princes on parade

Victoria and Albert first met in 1836; he was 16, she just 17. Albert and his brother Ernst were sent on holiday to England from Germany – at the same time as another of Victoria's match-making uncles, childless[2] King William IV, had invited his favoured candidates: Princes William and Alexander of the Netherlands.

Victoria met them all, and was most impressed by Albert:

'[He] is extremely handsome…his eyes are large and blue, and he has a beautiful nose and a very sweet mouth with fine teeth but the charm of his countenance is his expression, which is delightful.'

---

2. *Legally childless, that is. William IV had ten children from his long-term love affair with actress Dorothea Jordan.*

Victoria realised, too, that Albert was not just a pretty face: 'He has every quality that could be desired to make me happy.'

So why the wait? Events, dear reader, events. The very next year, in 1837, Victoria became queen. Determined to 'do my utmost to fulfil my duty to my country', she put all thoughts of marriage from her mind for a while. Two years later, in July 1839, she told King Leopold, who was urging another meeting with Prince Albert, that she wanted to be just good friends with him.

Love finds a way

Prince Albert came to Britain on 10 October that year, and the rest, as they say, is history. It was only their second meeting, but Victoria was soon head over heels in love. Albert, she realised, was 'beautiful' – 'and perfection in every way'. Five days later, she proposed,[3] saying 'that it would make me too happy if he would consent to what I wished'. Four months later, on 10 February 1840, they married.

Was Albert to be congratulated on winning the hand of the most powerful woman in the world? Victoria thought not. Tactfully, she recorded a private promise in her journal: 'I will strive to make him feel as little as possible the great sacrifice he has made!'

3. *as royal protocol demanded. Whatever his feelings might have been towards Victoria, Prince Albert was not allowed to propose to her.*

Right royal scandals

Sad to say, many other royal couples managed their love lives much less happily.

In their quest for romance, German **Princess Sophia Dorothea of Celle** and her husband, **Prince George of Hanover**,[4] stirred up Europe-wide scandals between them.

George and Sophia's marriage started very badly. In 1682, when they first met, the princess fainted clean away. After that, she called George 'Pig Face' and made it clear that she detested him. It's only fair to add that the bridegroom himself was not keen on the match; however, as his own mother remarked, 'One hundred thousand thalers a year[5] have tempted him as they would have tempted anyone else.'

Doing her royal duty – but still proclaiming her disgust – Sophia bore her husband two children (including the future British king George II) but then sought love in the arms

4. Sophia's cousin, the future King George I of England.
5. the bride's dowry (see page 43); the settlement also added the duchy belonging to Sophia's family to George's lands in Germany.

of a handsome Swedish army officer, Count Philip von Königsmarck. One evening in 1694, while George was away, the count was spotted entering the royal palace in Hanover. It was not his first visit. Later that night, he mysteriously disappeared – for ever!

Sophia's rooms were searched, and loving letters from the count were found hidden there. George claimed to be outraged, and demanded a divorce. It was quickly organised and Sophia – deeply disgraced – was locked up in one of George's castles for the rest of her life. She was not allowed to see her children, was banned from remarrying – and, so ghoulish rumours said, the body of her dead lover, the count, was buried, to torment her, under the floorboards of her prison.

When George arrived in England in 1714 to take up his newly inherited position as king, he brought his favourite mistress, not his wife, with him. Nicknamed 'the Maypole' by George's English courtiers, Melusine von der Schulenberg was a 'very tall, lean, ill-favoured lady', but she had been George's companion (along with several others) for 27 years.

A shining example?

Apart from rare, happily married royals, we have to turn back to Tudor times to find a princess who organised her own love life – and dealt with two extremely powerful kings – with exemplary tact and diplomacy. She also managed to marry the man she really loved – a rare pleasure for past royals.

Princess Mary Rose Tudor was the sister of England's King Henry VIII. Like him (when he was young), she was tall, golden-haired and strikingly attractive. She was also well educated and strong-willed. From childhood, she knew that she was destined to be married off to a great European ruler. Betrothals had been discussed, and come to nothing, since she was 3 years old. But in 1514, when Mary Rose was just 19, Henry finally chose a husband for her, for the usual political reasons. The eager groom was Louis XII, king of France – old (well, 52),[6] diseased, decrepit, and to some, disgusting!

6. By that age, many 16th-century people had lost their teeth, were stooped and wrinkled, and suffered from degenerative diseases such as osteoarthritis. The king was also afflicted by terribly painful gout, and possibly had either leprosy or a chronic sexually transmitted infection.

What a bargain!

Faced with such a husband, other princesses might have wept, or screamed, or stamped their feet and shouted. But Mary Rose was wise. Perhaps consoling herself with reports that her bridegroom-to-be was a considerate and kindly man – his plans to help the poor had earned him the nickname 'Father of his People' – and with the thought that she would become queen of the richest nation in Europe (Louis had already sent gifts of magnificent pearls and diamonds), Mary Rose agreed to the marriage. But only on one condition. If – when – old King Louis died, she would be free to choose her next husband.

He soon died (the marriage lasted only 82 days), and Mary Rose remarried. Although King Henry was not happy with the plan,[7] Mary Rose wed the man she loved, retired from royal marriage duties and politics at the royal court, and lived, fairly peacefully and happily, in the quiet Suffolk countryside.

7. *Mary's husband, Charles Brandon, duke of Suffolk, had been working as Henry's confidential ambassador in France. Henry felt betrayed.*

Few royal men or women could behave with such self-control and composure as Mary Rose Tudor – or expect to have such good luck. King Henry might well have gone back on his promise, and could even have executed her for disobeying his wishes if she refused to marry in the way he wanted for a second time.

Q. Which queen refused to wed?

A. Queen Elizabeth I of England (reigned 1558–1603). Proud to be known as the Virgin Queen, she stayed single so that no foreign king or English noble would win control of her kingdom. But she kept offering the hope of love or marriage in diplomatic negotiations with foreign princes, and flirted with hopeful English courtiers to keep them loyal.

Love, love, love

By the 20th century, royal rules about love and marriage were becoming more relaxed. This was partly due to the example set by Queen Victoria, but mostly to less hypocritical and more tolerant attitudes in society as a whole. Ideas about marriage were changing fast among ordinary men and women. And love, as entertainment, was all around – as gossip, in advertisements, on the radio, in novels and newpapers.

Yet paradoxically, at the same time as crowds gazed admiringly at photos of celebrity weddings, sighed over Hollywood's romantic films, or danced to the latest love songs from jazz bands and crooners, they were also getting divorced – or living together unwed – at a far greater rate than ever before.

However, for royalty, there were still some limits, as one young king of England discovered…

The royal love affair of the century?

KING TO MARRY 'WALLY'
US Daily Mirror *headline*

It was probably a first for a royal father. But in 1929, England's King George V declared, 'I pray to God that my eldest son will never marry and have children.' To King George, it seemed as if celebrity playboy the **Prince of Wales** was just too thoughtless and self-indulgent to fulfil his royal responsibilites. And that was before the prince had even met a certain Mrs Bessie Wallis Simpson...

The couple became friends in 1931, and lovers in 1933. The royal family, the UK government and Church leaders were horrified. Mrs Simpson came from America, which was a republic. Her crisp, sassy manners, showy jewels and ultra-fashionable clothes appeared brash and unladylike. In contrast to the prince's earlier, more discreet mistresses, she, and he, seemed shameless. As a divorced woman, she could never marry him in the Church of England.[8] They would be shunned by 'decent' British society – plus quite a few devout commoners.

8. *of which the prince would be the head once he became king.*

If all this was not reason enough to suspect the prince's new lover (and his judgement in befriending her), the pair also had undesirable friends in the German Nazi Party.

All for love

Once George V died (in 1936) and the Prince of Wales became King Edward VIII, his affair with Mrs Simpson was no longer just a private pain for the British royal family. It provoked a national political crisis – and endless, embarrassing speculation in the international media. Millions of readers and viewers devoured details of the scandalous royal romance. Today, this is commonplace, but then it was unheard-of, and most unseemly.

In October 1936, Mrs Simpson's second divorce was finalised. The king made up his mind: he wanted to marry her – morganatically (see page 56), if need be. But this would require a new law, and the British Parliament was unwilling. Mrs Simpson offered to 'withdraw from a situation both unhappy and untenable', but the king could not bear to lose her. After less than a year on the throne, King Edward VIII announced, in an unprecedented royal broadcast, that he was giving up his kingdom for love.

Was he a victim or a villain? Some might say, a bit of both.

' For if a man be careful to breed horses and dogs of good kinds, how much more careful should he be for the breed of his own loins... '

King James VI and I of Scotland and England, Basilikon Doron (book of advice for his son and heir), 1599

' It's an occupational hazard of being a wife. '

Princess Anne's view of pregnancy; TV interview, 1981

CHAPTER five

AN HEIR AND A SPARE

🦁

Princess Anne (see facing page) was quite right. Until the very recent past, being married and having children were almost inevitably linked together. A family – especially a royal one – couldn't be a family unless it had children. Without offspring to pass on the family genes – and name, rank, titles, property and power – a royal dynasty could no longer continue. It would become extinct – just a memory.

Apart from defending his realm, a king's first royal duty was to sire an heir to rule after him. Producing live, healthy – and legitimate – children to inherit their father's crown was even more important for queens. A royal woman who could not or would not have children was considered a failure – by the public and, often, by herself.

Q. Which king and queen had 16 children?

A. Devoted couple King Edward I of England and Queen Eleanor of Castile. Of their 11 daughters and 5 sons, 7 girls and one boy (later Edward II) survived. When Eleanor died aged 54, in 1290, Henry had 12 memorial crosses built to mark the places where her coffin rested each night on its long journey from Nottinghamshire to the royal burial place at Westminster Abbey.

Perpetually pregnant

Few queens tried harder to produce an heir, or suffered more tragic bereavements, than England's **Queen Anne**. Married aged 18 in 1683 to a Danish soldier-prince, she became pregnant almost straight away – and every year thereafter until 1700. But Anne's first child was stillborn. Five living babies followed, together with at least 12 miscarriages. But none of poor Anne's sons or daughters survived childhood. The longest-lived, Prince William, passed away when he was 11 years old, with his distraught mother and father at his bedside.

Long years of unsuccessful childbearing, followed by the death of her husband in 1708, left Queen Anne badly scarred, emotionally and physically. She died weak and exhausted six years later, aged 49. One of the royal doctors summed up her feelings: 'Sleep was never more welcome to a weary traveller than death was to her.'

'Too dreadful'

Queen Victoria loved her husband and was devoted to her duties as a ruling constitutional monarch. But there was one royal – and wifely – responsibility that she really disliked: having babies. Her letters and journals are full of complaints, from the time of her very first pregnancy.

'I cannot understand how anyone can wish for such a thing, especially at the beginning of a marriage.'

'...the first two years of my marriage utterly spoilt...I could enjoy nothing, not travel or go about...'

Victoria's troublesome pregnancies even made her (temporarily) hate the man who had fathered her children. She admitted saying 'stupid things' when she was 'unwell' – including that she was 'miserable I ever married'. And, although Victoria was a loving mother to all her nine children, she was never, ever, fond of newborn babies:

'An ugly baby is a very nasty object...that terrible frog-like action...'

In later years, Victoria also worried about how pregnancy and childbirth would affect her newly married daughters:

> 'When I think of a merry, happy, free young girl – and look at the ailing, aching state a young wife generally is doomed to – which you can't deny is the penalty of marriage...'

In fact, Queen Victoria shuddered, a woman – especially a royal bride – was always 'bodily and morally the husband's slave.' She was *not* amused.

Q. Why was there a double wedding – the only one in British royal history – in 1818?

A. To produce more heirs in a hurry. After Princess Charlotte died unexpectedly that year, there were no legitimate children to succeed her father, the Prince Regent. So three of her uncles (who all had mistresses) and one maiden aunt got married straight away. Two of them, Prince William of Clarence and Prince Edward of Kent, chose the same day and place.

Who's to blame?

Queen Anne (see page 99) believed that her failure to provide her country with an heir was God's punishment; she had once plotted against her father.[1] And it was usually queens who took the blame if a royal couple had no children. Until the 20th century, medical reasons for infertility were not fully understood; kings, like ordinary men, simply did not believe that the fault might sometimes lie with *their* biology.

Longing for love

For seven years after her marriage in 1770, young, healthy Queen Marie Antoinette endured taunts and scoldings – from her mother, Empress Maria Theresa of Austria, and from the courtiers of her husband, French King Louis XVI. Why had she not yet had children? Was she cold and selfish? Had she upset her husband, the king? Was she not trying hard enough, by 'caressing and cajoling', to make him make love to her?

1. *In 1688 Anne had backed plans by Protestant politicians to remove her father, Catholic James II, from the throne.*

It seemed quite clear – to all Europe! – that Marie Antoinette was a failure, as a woman and a wife – and also as a royal Austrian. If she could not provide the king with an heir, he might send her back to her homeland. The disgrace, to Marie Antoinette's family and her nation, would be unbearable.

It was, the Austrians decided, time to take action. In 1777 Marie Antoinette's brother (now Emperor Joseph II) arrived in France on a very delicate mission. Man to man, he spoke to King Louis, encouraging and reassuring him. Yes, the king faced certain medical problems in performing his marital duties, but they could be overcome. Joseph also scolded his sister – though by letter, not in person. She was to give up extravagant shopping, and nights out with flirtatious, fun-loving friends. Instead she must devote herself to the king, welcoming him to her bed and wooing him with 'charm and friendliness'.

Joseph's wise words did the trick. Within months, a delighted Marie Antoinette announced that she was pregnant. (Charmingly, she did this by telling her husband that 'one of your majesty's subjects' had just kicked her in the belly.) She gave her delighted husband – and (less enthusiastic) France – a daughter and two sons.

Top breeders prefer...

To try to make sure of the best chance of getting an heir, kings often asked for reports on the likely childbearing abilities of prospective brides.

Using rather agricultural language, King **James VI and I** (see page 96) advised his son to choose 'a wife of a whole and clean race,[2] not subject to hereditary sicknesses, either of the soul or of the body'.

In 1505, King **Henry VII** studiously asked his ambassadors to describe both the hips and 'the breasts or pappes' of the young (27), widowed Queen Joan of Naples. (The latter were, so the envoy said, 'somewhat great and full...trussed somewhat high, after the manner [fashion] of the country'.)

2. race: breed, as in breeds of dogs or horses.

If you think these concerns with fertility sound hopelessly quaint and old-fashioned, remember that American film star **Grace Kelly** had to be examined by a doctor before her planned marriage to Prince Rainier of Monaco could go ahead in 1955.

Royal husbands have also felt slighted when their duties (and even identities) – apart from being the successful father of heirs – have been overlooked or slighted.

One of straight-talking **Prince Philip**'s most famously forthright remarks was his reaction in 1952 to the suggestion[3] that his children with Queen Elizabeth II should be given her family surname, Windsor. Philip is said to have exclaimed:

> 'I am nothing but a bloody amoeba!
> I am the only man in the country not allowed
> to give his name to his own children.'

In 1960, after Queen Mary died, Queen Elizabeth II tactfully changed the royal surname to Mountbatten-Windsor.

3. *by Britain's dowager Queen Mary (Queen Elizabeth II's grandmother) and Prime Minister Winston Churchill.*

Yours faithfully

In addition to being 'good breeding stock', royal wives were expected to be utterly faithful to their husbands. As the Roman proverb declared, 'Caesar's wife must be above suspicion.' As 18th-century English dictionary-writer Dr Johnson explained: 'Upon that [female chastity] all property in the world depends.' If there was the slightest suspicion that a royal heir was not the son of his official father, then he would not be accepted by his subjects as their future king.

No safety in numbers

King Henry I (reigned 1154–1189) holds the record among English kings for fathering the largest number of children. With his first wife, Queen Edith, he had two sons and a daughter. He also had 20 (some say 24) illegitimate children with several different mistresses. Yet Henry left no male heir to rule after him. Both his lawful sons died while he was still alive; his unlawful sons could not inherit his kingdom. And when his daughter, Matilda, tried to claim her father's kingdom, there was civil war.

Bedpan baby

King James II also had many illegitimate children, but no lawful male heirs. After his first wife died, he married again, but his second wife Mary also failed to produce the longed-for son.

Early in 1688, in the middle of a dire political crisis, Mary announced that she was pregnant again. This surprised many people – Mary was old for motherhood, and not in good health – but in July, James's friends joyfully announced that she had given birth to a boy. However, the baby's arrival into this world was not witnessed – as was usual – by leading politicians, or by representatives of King James's daughters, who had been his heirs until then.

Their supporters – the majority of the English people – whispered that the baby was not James's, but had been smuggled into Queen Mary's bed in a warming pan. Parliament, the Protestant Church and the English army refused to support James, and he fled, with Mary and the baby, to France.

first and foremost

Though any baby born to a royal couple was welcome – it at least proved that they were capable of having children – a son was preferred. It was widely believed that women were by nature, temperament and biology unfit to rule; they could not fight or lead armies; they were weak, mentally or physically; they were not well educated; they were barred from senior positions in the Church; they were gentle and tender, not tough and resolute; they were at the mercy of their emotions (or weak from pregnancy); and they were easily tempted into folly, or swayed by evil advisors. Above all, in most of Europe, women could not, for most of their lives,[4] own property – let alone a kingdom.

4. Until the 19th century in most European nations, a woman's inherited property passed to her father if she was a child, or to her husband once she married. Only unmarried women or widows were free to control what they inherited.

Husband takes all

Therefore, although daughters were useful bargaining counters for fathers or brothers to marry off to make alliances, sons were needed to inherit a kingdom. If a ruler died without male heirs, then his eldest daughter's husband had the right to take over her possessions. This could, and did (as we have seen before), lead to situations where a woman inheriting the crown lost her independence, at least until the next heir was born.

These rules were the reason why England's King Henry VIII was so desperate to father a son to rule after him. Though few kings were quite so determined – or quite so murderous…

An heir for Henry

1503
Your problem? You're Prince Henry Tudor, second son of King Henry VII. A year ago, your big brother, Prince Arthur, died suddenly. Now your father's decided that you must marry Arthur's widow – your sister-in-law – Spanish Princess Catherine of Aragon. You're just 11 years old (she's 17), but you go through a betrothal ceremony with her.

1505
Henry VII changes his politics. He'd rather you wed a French princess, but dare not offend Spain. So your marriage will go ahead – so long as the Pope gives permission. Why the Pope? Because marrying your brother's wife is against Church law. Under pressure from Catherine's parents, the Pope agrees that you can. He's helped by Catherine, who swears that she's still a virgin. If so, your brother Arthur was never truly her husband.

1509
Your father dies. Now you are king – aged 17. You need an heir – and quickly! After just six weeks, you marry Catherine.

1520
After ten years of marriage you're beginning to despair. Catherine's been a loving (if gloomy) wife, but where are your hoped-for children? Only one daughter, Mary, has survived. Modern

scholars suggest that stress at the Tudor court made Catherine anorexic. But you – and she – think childlessness is God's punishment. You ask the Pope to undo his previous permission and declare your marriage invalid. Under pressure from Catherine's nephew, Emperor Charles V (see page 31), he refuses.

Never mind. You're at your peak – a tall, handsome, manly figure, well educated, athletic and musical. As one ambassador reports:

'His Majesty is the most handsomest potentate I have ever set eyes on: above the usual height, with an extremely fine calf to his leg and a round face so very beautiful it would become a pretty woman.'

1525
Still no heir, and Catherine has reached 40. She's not likely now to have a son – but you *have* met a fascinating young woman. Her name is Anne Boleyn. For more than six extremely frustrating years, she refuses to be your lover.

1532–3
Anne Boleyn finally gives in, after a secret royal marriage. Soon she is pregnant. What if her child is a boy? He must be born in wedlock! You marry Anne again, this time in public, and send Catherine of Aragon away – for ever.

1533
Under pressure, the Archbishop of Canterbury declares that your marriage to Catherine was

invalid, and that your marriage to Anne Boleyn is absolutely lawful. (This is a direct challenge to the authority of the Pope and the unity of the Catholic Church. It leads to religious upheavals, during which you become 'supreme head' of the Church in England.) Anne's baby is a girl (Elizabeth). You're *so* disappointed! Some say your personality changes – you become fierce and cruel – after a jousting accident. Around the same time, you probably develop type 2 diabetes. Your sporty physique balloons: your chest increases from 39 in (1 m) to 54 in (1.37 m); your weight rises to 28 stone (178 kg).

1536
Disaster! In January Anne Boleyn has a miscarriage. The child would have been a boy. You decide that Anne is a witch, and must go. In May, she's beheaded. The day before Anne dies, you betrothe yourself to a new bride – an English nobleman's daughter, Jane Seymour. In less than a fortnight, you marry her.

1537
Congratulations! Jane gives birth to a baby boy (Edward) – but dies of an infection 12 days later.

1540
In January, wife no. 4, Anne of Cleves (see pages 72–73), arrives in London. You're very disappointed. She's big and bonny, but her bouncy self-confidence and plain face do not attract you. Even so, you wed her – to send her home would cause an international political crisis. You suggest an annulment (a

declaration on legal and religious grounds that the marriage was never valid), on generous terms. Anne agrees, happily. You're free again, but your only son, Edward, is weak and feeble. You desperately need a spare heir.

1540
One of Anne's pretty teenage attendants has caught your eye. It's Katherine Howard, niece to the duke of Norfolk. You marry her in July.

1542
Katherine's young, so you have high hopes of an heir – but alas, she proves unfaithful. (That's what court gossips say – and you believe them.) Katherine's beheaded in February.

1543
Now you're 51, grossly fat, with ulcerated legs and all kinds of unpleasant diseases. But you don't give up hope. You persuade clever widow Katherine Parr to postpone her wedding to an old sweetheart, and marry you instead. She's more of a nurse than a wife, but still, while you can, you keep trying...

1547
It's over. You've gone to meet your Maker – and, who knows, the ghosts of those wives who've died before you. You leave a sickly son and two remarkable daughters. The boy, King Edward VI, will soon die (in 1553). Your eldest girl will reign, embittered and reviled, as 'Bloody Mary'. Your second daughter, Elizabeth, will be one of England's very greatest rulers.

' ...all arrayed like a
bride beautified and
adorned for
her husband... '

Revelations 21:2

CHAPTER SIX

HERE COMES THE BRIDE

No, not 'short, fat and wide' as the playground song has it, but dressed in the most sumptuous garments of her era. Even the poorest bride tried to look her best on her wedding day – to please her husband and bring credit to her family. So, with the wealth of whole kingdoms at their disposal, royal brides (and grooms) made extra-special efforts to delight and dazzle by displays of exquisite clothing and magnificent jewellery.

Q. *Why did Princess Diana have a splitting headache after her wedding?*

A. Because the glittering tiara that she wore was so heavy. An heirloom belonging to Diana's family, the Spencers, it was made from hundreds of large diamonds set in gold, in a pattern of tulips and star-flowers.

But royal brides had to please other people as well as their husbands. Huge crowds thronging the streets – and, from the 19th century onwards, worldwide audiences of newspaper readers, radio listeners or TV viewers[1] – would also be taking notice. By the 21st century, images of royal weddings were being flashed round the world in seconds by electronic media. Praise or criticism came just as quickly. Looking richly dressed and 'radiant' (the commentators' favourite way of describing all brides) might be a real royal pleasure, but it also became a demanding duty.

1. The first newsreel of a royal wedding was in 1923; the first live radio broadcast, 1947. The first British royal wedding to be televised live was Princess Margaret's in 1960.

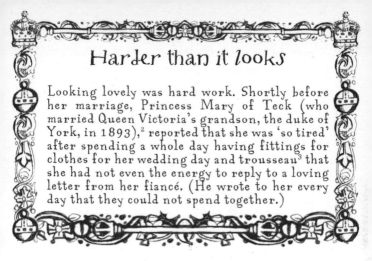

Harder than it looks

Looking lovely was hard work. Shortly before her marriage, Princess Mary of Teck (who married Queen Victoria's grandson, the duke of York, in 1893),[2] reported that she was 'so tired' after spending a whole day having fittings for clothes for her wedding day and trousseau[3] that she had not even the energy to reply to a loving letter from her fiancé. (He wrote to her every day that they could not spend together.)

fairytale frocks

Come and join those watching crowds! Travel back in time to watch a royal fashion parade. Most royal brides liked to be right up to date in the styles that they chose for their weddings; some even hoped to be fashion leaders. They chose frocks that proudly displayed their royal power and status, or else they escaped, like Princess Diana, into a fashion fairyland of romance and fantasy.

2. *He later became King George V, and she Queen Mary.*
3. *trousseau: the collection of clothes to be worn by a young married woman. Princess Mary's trousseau included at least 40 outdoor costumes, 15 ballgowns, 5 tea gowns and dozens of hats, gloves and shoes.*

Royal bridegrooms also liked to dress to impress. Until the late 19th century, their clothes were as stylish and trend-setting as their brides'. After that, it became the royal male fashion to wear splendid but very conventional full-dress military uniform – together with as many medals, sashes, badges of honour and elaborate gold braids as their proud, manly bosoms had room for. Only a few, like the duke of Edinburgh at his wedding in 1947, showed elegant restraint. He wore naval uniform with medal ribbons earned on active wartime service, and just two jewelled stars: from the highest orders of chivalry in his homeland, Greece, and his newly adopted country, Britain.

Enough of that, for riding towards us right now we have:

1191 The king himself, **Richard I** (the Lionheart). Excuse me while I cheer: Hooray! Hooray! Now, what is he wearing? Oh, magnificent! – rose-pink heavy silk, embroidered with silver suns and golden moons, a blood-red velvet cap, and gold boots with silver spurs.

Ah! Look! Here comes our first bride. It's one of the very few medieval princesses whose clothes we know about. Most medieval chronicles were written by monks, who claimed that women were 'the gateway to hell' and that fashionable clothes were even more unspeakable.

c.1400 My word, look at this! A medieval queen's golden gala gown – the only one still surviving today![4] Long-sleeved, tight-fitting, with amazing full, sweeping skirts, it's made of rich red silk interwoven with an all-over pattern in threads of real gold. It probably belonged to **Queen Margareta Valdemarsdotter** of Sweden, and, according to tradition, it might even be her wedding gown!

1436 How tiny she is! Yes, she's only 11. It's Scottish **Princess Margaret**, on her way to marry French prince Louis. She's wearing cloth of gold and a golden crown; he's dressed in grey-blue velvet with shiny gold embroidery, and carries a jewelled sword.

4. in Uppsala cathedral, Sweden.

1468 Now, who is this? Ah, **Margaret** of rich, go-ahead Burgundy. Very smart and refined! White and gold brocade, trimmed with pure white ermine.

1501 Now we're in Tudor times. Oh – what have we here? Spanish princess **Catherine of Aragon**, bride of Prince Arthur (see pages 110–111). That must be a Spanish design she's wearing. Her bell-shaped long skirt – white satin – is stretched out over stiffened hoops; I believe they call it a *farthingale*. And she has a veil: more white silk, trimmed with gold and jewels. See, the Prince is dressed in white, to match her.

1540 Fourth time lucky, perhaps? Well, we hope so, and **King Henry VIII** certainly looks like a happy, confident and supremely royal bridegroom. Gold and silver doublet, cloak of crimson trimmed with silver, and a stupendous diamond necklace. **Anne of Cleves** – a tall lass – wears cloth of gold embroidered with pearls, and a jewelled coronet.

1544 Ah! The bride wears black velvet. Not because she, **Queen Mary Tudor**, feels miserable, but because the dark cloth is a wonderful backdrop for all the amazing jewels that have been sewn on to it. By contrast her bridegroom, Spanish **King Philip I**, wears white and blood-red: white breeches and doublet and a long coat of crimson silk, velvet and cloth of gold, trimmed with gold and pearls. Very, very fine, sire!

1588 Well, here we are in France, for what must be the biggest fashion shock of the century! The young **Mary, Queen of Scots** has just married the Dauphin (crown prince) – and she's worn white, the French colour of death and mourning. That's not to say she didn't look good (she did: she chose white because it suited her). And there was plenty of colour in her crown: it sparkled with sapphires, rubies, pearls and massive diamonds. Even so, many French people fear that this royal fashion will bring bad luck. Only time will tell…

1612 Now there's a new dynasty, the Stuarts, on the throne of England. And its head, King James I (who's also James VI of Scots), has arranged a marriage for his daughter, **Princess Elizabeth**, to Palatine (German) Emperor Frederick. She's wearing a full-skirted, tight-waisted white satin dress absolutely dripping with diamonds. Wow, Your Royal Highness!

1745 Another century, many more royal weddings – and now most brides are dressed in silver. Brocade, lace, net, gauzy tissue – everywhere it glitters and sparkles. Look, here's **Princess Catherine**, soon to be the mighty empress of Russia. Her wedding dress is made of silver cloth, with extra silver embroidery. With a silver lace cloak on top, the whole ensemble must be tremendously heavy. They say that her mother-in-law wanted Catherine to cover her glossy black hair with fashionable silver-grey powder, but the bride refused. Quite understandable, young lady!

1840 It's the great queen herself: **Victoria**! Not the dumpy figure dressed all in black that we remember from her later years, but a young, pretty bride in a charming, low-necked, full-skirted frock of plain white satin. It's trimmed with priceless lace, but otherwise it looks so fresh and simple. No cloth of gold or silver. No jewelled embroidery. No long, cumbersome train. What a fashion revolution!

1893 If ever there was a fashion-plate bride, it's **Princess Mary** (often known as May), new wife of the Prince of Wales. She's tall, with an hourglass figure (those corsets can't be comfortable), and her dress is truly regal. The pale cream (and silver!) silk cloth has been specially woven with patterns of British roses, shamrocks and thistles. But oh dear! What a tragic fashion note is struck by her grandmother-in-law, Queen Victoria. She's still wearing widow's black, but with the veil she wore at her own wedding.

1923 Now here's a dress that's right up to the minute in style, but – we wonder – will future generations find it flattering? It's made for shy, smiling **Lady Elizabeth Bowes-Lyon**,[5] who's marrying the duke of York.[6] She's chosen a long, very straight, loose – some say shapeless – dress, following the trend set by corsetless 'flappers'. It's in ivory silk, and down the front there are panels of tiny, tiny beads plus gold and silver embroidery.

1947 Here's perhaps the most romantic wedding dress of them all, made for **Princess Elizabeth**.[7] It's an exquisite work of art, glamorous and slim-fitting, in heavy silk satin, embroidered with 10,000 pearls and countless sparkling crystals. But what makes it extra-special is the hope of peace and plenty that its embroidered stars, flowers and ears of wheat symbolise for Britain. The country and its people are still staggering after six years of a terrible world war.

5. *later Queen Elizabeth the Queen Mother.*
6. *later King George VI.*
7. *later Queen Elizabeth II.*

Under the veil

Like wedding dresses today, clothing for past royal weddings was influenced by tradition as well as fashion.

Royal bridal veils were first recorded in Assyrian and Hebrew lands over 3,000 years ago, as signs of female modesty and purity. They were sometimes also, as later in ancient Rome, magic protection against evil spirits that might attack a young woman as she passed – dangerously! – from the virginal to the married state.

As a similar sign, medieval royal brides wore their long hair flowing loose over their shoulders, like innocent little girls. (Many *were* little girls, of course.) They might also wear a veil, or a jewelled headdress, or a coronet.

In 1297 King Edward I of England paid for a gold circlet set with pearls, emeralds and rubies for his daughter **Elizabeth** to wear.

By the 1640s a royal bride's hair was tied up with ribbons, not dishevelled about her shoulders as in former times. Gold circlets were still worn until around 1800, but were now trimmed with diamonds and towering ostrich plumes.

In 1795, when sophisticated (and allegedly promiscuous) bride **Princess Caroline of Brunswick** chose to wear her long curls flowing free, the sight was greeted with ridicule.

By the 19th century, plumes and long hair had disappeared, and veils (with upswept tresses) once again became popular – for bridesmaids as well as brides. Royal veils were now made of delicate handcrafted lace, and usually topped with wreaths of real orange blossom.

In 1840, **Queen Victoria**'s short lace veil, worn at the back of the head, framed her face very prettily.

However, the 1920s style favoured by **Princess Mary**, daughter of King George V, and all her bridesmaids, was much less becoming. They wore floor-length lace 'curtains' pulled low down on the forehead and held in place with a headband – almost like the traditional Middle Eastern *keffiyeh*.

From the 1940s, most royal brides – including **Princess Elizabeth**, **Princess Margaret** and **Princess Anne** – have preferred simple, transparent veils of whisper-light silk tulle. And they've topped these with priceless heirloom diamond tiaras.

Make mine myrtle

Other royal bridal traditions were restricted to certain families. For example, all British royal brides descended from Queen Victoria have included among their wedding flowers a sprig of myrtle[8] from the bush growing in Queen Victoria's garden on the Isle of Wight. It grew from a cutting brought by Prince Albert from Coburg in Germany, which he presented to Victoria for her bouquet.

8. *a plant with sweet-smelling leaves, traditionally a symbol of love and marriage.*

With this ring...

Since ancient Egyptian times, rings – which have no beginning and no end – have been a sign of undying love. The Romans were probably the first to exchange betrothal or engagement rings – usually in the shape of clasped hands, another symbol of everlasting friendship. Roman rulers wore their betrothal rings on the fourth finger of the left hand, because they believed that a vein ran from there directly to the heart. Their wedding rings were often made of iron – a metal that would last.

Later, medieval kings and queens wore their betrothal and wedding rings on the first fingers of their right or left hands. (That custom is forgotten today.) The rings they exchanged were made of gold, sometimes set with sapphires or rubies.

In 1477, Hapsburg **Prince Maximilian** (see pages 37–38) was the first-known royal to offer his fiancée, **Mary of Burgundy**, a ring embellished with diamonds. Rough diamonds could not be cut and polished to brilliancy in the Middle Ages, so they were not normally as highly prized as coloured stones. But Maximilian linked their enduring qualities to his promise of lasting love.

In 1554, **Mary Tudor** chose to be married with a plain and simple gold ring 'like lasses used to be'.

The Catholic Church, to which she was devoted, taught (until 1614) that wedding rings should be worn on the right hand. But from 1549 England's religious reformers demanded the left hand instead. They also recommended rings carved inside with stern mottoes, such as 'Observe wedlock'.

In 1840, **Queen Victoria**'s engagement ring was shaped like a snake – another ancient Roman symbol of eternal love. Made of yellow gold, its head was set with emeralds, Queen Victoria's birthstone.

In 1923, the **duchess of York** chose an engagement ring set with sapphires and diamonds. Later, as a widow (the Queen Mother), in the 1950s, she began to wear a large pearl and diamond ring instead.

In 1936, the **duke of Windsor** gave **Mrs Simpson** an engagement ring with a single magnificent square-cut emerald.

In 1947, **Prince Philip**'s family, although royal, did not have much ready money. So the engagement ring he gave **Princess Elizabeth** was fashioned using stones from a tiara inherited by his mother, Princess Andrew of Greece. The prince designed the ring himself; it consists of a large (3-carat) square diamond, surrounded by ten smaller diamonds, all set in platinum. It is rumoured that if the Queen is annoyed, she twists the ring round on her finger.

Sapphire sensation

In 2010, royal-watchers were astonished to see the famous deep-blue 18-carat sapphire and diamond engagement ring, formerly worn by the late Princess Diana, sparkling on the fourth finger of **Prince William of Wales**'s new fiancée. Was this royal recycling? Why not something new? All but the hardest hearts melted when Prince William offered a very touching explanation: it was one way of making sure that his beloved mother 'did not miss out' on the joy and excitement of her eldest son's wedding.

No more where that came from

In 1999, the only mine in Wales that produced rare rose-tinted Welsh gold – six times more costly than ordinary gold – closed for ever. Since 1923, Welsh gold has been used to make wedding rings for British royalty, including Queen Elizabeth the Queen Mother, Princess Margaret, Princess Diana and the duchess of Cornwall. However, the Queen still owns enough Welsh gold to make (just) a few more royal rings.

A few fashion follies

1297 Thirty-four tailors worked nonstop for four days and four nights to complete the wedding dress for **Princess Elizabeth**, daughter of King Edward I of England.

1501 **King James IV** of Scotland chose to wear rather alarming bright blood-red hose to his wedding.

1625 When **King Charles I** of England met his bride **Princess Henrietta Maria**, he peered under her skirts. She was taller than he expected! Was she wearing heels? No, she wasn't! 'Sire, I stand upon my own feet', she said.

1661 A French-style, gilt-embroidered suit (long coat and knee-breeches) worn by the future **James II**, possibly for his first wedding, still survives in the Victoria & Albert Museum in London.

1745 When **Princess Marie Antoinette** arrived at the border between Austria and France on the way to her wedding, she was made to change out of all her Austrian clothes before crossing into her new country, and put on French fashions.

1736 and **1761** German **Princesses Augusta and Charlotte** had never seen their wedding dresses until it was time to put them on. They were chosen by their future husbands' advisors in England.

1840 Queen Victoria herself designed the dresses for her 12 bridesmaids. They were all made of white silk, adorned with pure white roses.

1862 Princess Alice, Queen Victoria's daughter, had to change into dark, sombre clothes right after her wedding ceremony. The royal court was still in deep mourning after the death of her father, Prince Albert, the previous year.

1863 Princess Alexandra of Denmark trimmed her light, lacy wedding gown with so much fresh, sweet-smelling orange blossom that some people joked that she looked like a walking shrubbery.

1934 The silk and silver tissue used to make Greek **Princess Marina**'s wedding dress was so fragile that dressmakers started work only two weeks before the wedding. The finished garment would not be strong enough to survive long storage.

1936 Mrs Simpson did not wear white for her wedding to the duke of Windsor. Her dress was in a pale, elegant, misty shade, nicknamed 'Wallis blue' in her honour.

1947 A fashion crisis loomed when it was feared that the silk used to make **Princess Elizabeth**'s wedding dress might have come from Japanese silkworms.[9] The panic died down after it was revealed that it had come instead from silkworms of Chinese origin, living in Kent.

1955 Princess Grace's wedding dress was created not by by a top fashion house but, appropriately enough, by a Hollywood costume designer.

1960 Almost 98 feet (30 metres) of silk organza fabric were used to make the full-skirted dress worn by the very petite **Princess Margaret.**

1981 The train of **Princess Diana**'s wedding dress was a royal-record-breaking 25 feet (7.6 metres) long. As the whole world noticed, it could not fit comfortably into her royal horse-drawn carriage, and emerged creased and crumpled.

2005 The **duchess of Cornwall** (Prince Charles's second wife) wore two different wedding outfits on the same day: first a short silk coat and day dress for the civil ceremony, then a floor-length pale blue and gold outfit, with a fantastic feather fascinator, for the church blessing afterwards.

9. *Until two years before the wedding, Britain had been at war with Japan.*

> **6 Magnificent, preposterous, and overblown 9**

Historian David Starkey, describing the ceremonial at Prince Charles and Princess Diana's wedding, 1981

> **6 The Abbey is where our history is. 9**

Visitor to Westminster Abbey, 2010

> **6 A cat may look at a king. 9**

Traditional saying

CHAPTER SEVEN

GET ME TO THE CHURCH...

❧

In 1548 Princess Anna, aged 16, set off on a long overland journey – it would take weeks – to meet and be married to the husband chosen for her by her family. She came from Denmark; he lived in Saxony in south-east Germany. Anna's parents, King Christian III and Queen Dorothea of Denmark, hoped that her journey would be comfortable. But just as – or maybe even more – important, they were determined to take this opportunity of a grand royal marriage to show all Europe just how splendid and civilised a country the bride was leaving behind her. Denmark was not a quiet, Nordic backwater! No – like Anna's marriage journey, it was rich and proud.

The king and queen took no chances. Everything was carefully planned – from the number of knights leading the procession (13 rows, riding three abreast), to the uniforms (velvet, but nothing too ostentatious) worn by top nobles, their servants – and their horses. The bride herself travelled in a gold-painted carriage, with her mother's carriage and two extra carriages[1] (a wedding gift) following behind. Then came the ladies-in-waiting, a great many servants – from cooks to baggage-handlers – plus a crowd of senior royal employees, each with special duties: a doctor, a pharmacist, several tailors, scribes and messengers, and a priest. There were heavy waggons laden with wedding presents, and a troop of musicians. These included lute-players for quiet, indoor music, and trumpet players for the opposite kind of sound. Plus two parrots.

1. the equivalent of limousines today.

What a spectacle!

We do not know how Princess Anna felt on her long journey, or how other young royal brides responded to the noisy, rowdy, smelly crowds who flocked to gawp at them, or to the elaborate tableaux, fancy-dress pageants, dangerous tournaments, drunken dancing, alarming illuminations and other public displays that greeted their arrival. These must sometimes have been rather intimidating:

In 1177 the streets of Palermo, Sicily, were so brightly lit with flares and braziers to welcome **Princess Joan**[2] that it looked as if the whole city had caught fire and was burning.

In 1445 the citizens of London welcomed French **Princess Marguerite of Anjou**[3] with well-meant but perhaps not very encouraging Bible-story pageants, including the Foolish Virgins, and the Day of Judgement, complete with Hell.

2. *daughter of England's King Henry II.*
3. *bride of King Henry VI of England.*

Even so, some royal brides apparently took everything in their stride:

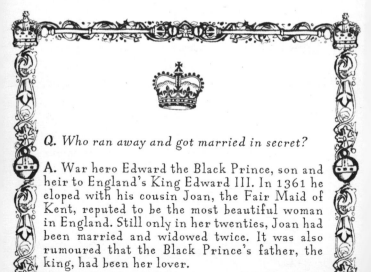 In 1503, after travelling – cushioned by bearskins – all the way to Scotland, young **Margaret Tudor**'s wedding procession was ambushed by her impatient husband-to-be, King James IV. The young couple ended up peacefully listening to music and playing cards together.

Q. Who ran away and got married in secret?

A. War hero Edward the Black Prince, son and heir to England's King Edward III. In 1361 he eloped with his cousin Joan, the Fair Maid of Kent, reputed to be the most beautiful woman in England. Still only in her twenties, Joan had been married and widowed twice. It was also rumoured that the Black Prince's father, the king, had been her lover.

Happy holidays?

For the spectators, a royal wedding progress was an excuse for merry-making – or at least for stopping their work for a while to stand and stare – even if they did have to make fools of themselves with flowers, on royal officials' orders.

In 1445, French **Princess Marguerite of Anjou** was – so chroniclers said – welcomed to England by the rough peasants working alongside her route from the south coast to London. They wore daisies – Marguerite means 'daisy' in French. But English peasants did not speak French – so which royal servants organised this display, and how? Or was the chronicler just inventing a pretty story?

Join the crowd

For **Queen Victoria**'s wedding in 1840, Londoners dragged kitchen tables into the streets, to stand on to get a better view of the wedding procession. A few enterprising families made a tidy profit by renting them out to wealthier bystanders.

Other spectators climbed trees in St James's Park, close to Queen Victoria's royal home. The branches broke, and the climbers fell into the crowd below. There were not *too* many casualties…

By the time that the **Prince of Wales** wed **Princess Mary** in 1893, the London area was very well provided with railways. Operating companies ran hundreds of special excursion trains to bring spectators from the suburbs. Just one line, the Metropolitan, carried over half a million (very precisely, they claimed 514,727 passengers).

At **Princess Elizabeth**'s wedding in 1947, sweets, periscopes, flowers and other souvenirs were on sale to keep the waiting crowds happy.

It was estimated that around 2 million men, women and children lined London's streets to catch a glimpse of the wedding of **Prince Charles** and **Princess Diana** in 1981. Some camped out on the pavement for days beforehand. Around 750 million TV viewers watched the event live, worldwide.

Q. Which mighty queen promised to obey her husband?

A. Queen Victoria, in 1840. Traditionally, a bride promised to obey her husband as part of her wedding vows.

The archbishop of Canterbury, no less, asked Victoria whether she would like to leave the word out of her promise. She refused.

Where, oh where?

For over a thousand years, royal weddings in Europe have been Christian ceremonies, but the choice of marriage venues has varied widely, from historic holy places to private dining rooms. Some weddings have been quick, quiet, even secret; others have grown into huge public ceremonials.

Over 3,500 guests attended the 1981 wedding of the **Prince of Wales and Princess Diana**, at St Paul's Cathedral in London. What a contrast with Queen Victoria's wedding of 1840, in the Chapel Royal at St James's Palace, also in London, which has room for only 100.

More modest still was the wedding of Queen Victoria's daughter, **Princess Alice**, to Prince Louis of Hesse, celebrated – if that is the word – in 1862, less than a year after Victoria's husband Prince Albert had died. The queen insisted that the ceremony should be strictly private – so it was held in the dining room of the royal family's summer home, Osborne House, on the Isle of Wight.

One of the biggest, most extravagant and most public royal weddings took place in 1501 between **Prince Arthur**, son of the first Tudor king Henry VII, and **Catherine of Aragon**, daughter of the grand and glorious Spanish ruling dynasty. The Tudors had seized power after a bloody civil war; many, rich and poor, still saw them as upstarts with no real right to rule. In the same way as royal advisors hoped that Prince Charles and Princess Diana's 'fairytale' celebration would help revive interest in the 20th-century monarchy, Henry VII hoped that a prestigious royal wedding would make his family look more legitimate.

Prince Arthur wed Princess Catherine at Old St Paul's Cathedral.[4] It was claimed that half the inhabitants of London – around 20,000 people – turned out for the occasion. The couple entered the cathedral along a raised wooden walkway almost 656 feet (200 metres) long, and exchanged their vows on a high wooden platform in the middle of the nave, so everyone could see them.

4. *Destroyed in the Great Fire of 1666, it was even bigger than Wren's huge building which replaced it.*

Royal Peculiar

Westminster Abbey, a magnificent church founded in 1065 by England's only royal saint, Edward the Confessor (ruled 1042–1066), stands right at the heart of London. The Houses of Parliament are close by, and so is the modern royal residence of Buckingham Palace. Traditionally, the Abbey has been the place where English, then British, kings and queens were crowned, and where many were buried.

In legal terms, the Abbey is a Royal Peculiar; it belongs to the monarch, not to the Church. But until the 20th century it was very rarely used for royal weddings.

That custom was changed in 1919, by Princess Patricia, one of Queen Victoria's grand-children. She was the first royal bride to wed there for several hundred years. (The very first was Princess Matilda of Scotland, who married King Henry I of England in 1100.)

Princess Patsy (as she was known) was probably attracted by the Abbey's size (it can seat over 2,000 guests) and central location, as well as by its history and beauty. Her choice also fitted in with King George V's decision, in 1917, to make the monarchy more British[5] – and much more publicly visible.

5. He changed the royal family's surname from Saxe-Coburg-Gotha to Windsor, and his royal relatives' name from Battenburg to Mountbatten.

Since 1919 most royal weddings have been held at the Abbey, including:

1922 Princess Mary, daughter of King George V, to Viscount Lascelles

1923 Lady Elizabeth Bowes-Lyon to Prince Albert, duke of York

1947 Princess Elizabeth to Lieutenant (formerly Prince) Philip Mountbatten, duke of Edinburgh

1960 Princess Margaret to Antony Armstrong-Jones (later earl of Snowdon)

1963 Princess Alexandra to the Hon. Angus Ogilvy

1973 Princess Anne to Captain Mark Phillips

1986 Prince Andrew to Sarah Ferguson.

flowers for the fallen

In a graceful gesture, copied by many later royal brides, **Lady Elizabeth Bowes-Lyon** left her wedding bouquet on the tomb of the Unknown Warrior in Westminster Abbey. This grave marked the resting place of an anonymous Allied soldier killed in World War I. His remains had been moved to the Abbey, with full military honours, in 1920, just three years before the wedding.

No publicity!

Some royal weddings were small and private, because the royal family – or a royal individual – was unpopular:

When, in 1794, the **Prince of Wales** told his father, George III, that he wanted to marry Princess Caroline of Brunswick, the British ambassador in Berlin warned that Caroline would 'ensure the misery' of the Prince, rather than make him happy. (The ambassador turned out to be right; see pages 173–174.)

Some weddings were hurried through, on questionable grounds, for political reasons:

Viking warlord (later king) **Cnut** of Denmark seized control of England in 1017. One of his first acts (after murdering the heir to the throne) was to marry Emma, the widow of English King Æthelred II. By this hasty wedding, Cnut hoped to stop the English people – and Emma's brother, the powerful duke of Normandy – from challenging his takeover.

Some weddings would have caused religious controversy if they had been publicised:

In 1662 **King Charles II** of England got married twice – in Portsmouth, of all places. He hurried there to meet the ship carrying his bride, Portuguese Princess Catherine of Braganza. She was a Roman Catholic, and so they had small, quick, quiet ceremonies, one Catholic and one Protestant.

And some royal marriages were simply an embarrassment, to be concealed rather than celebrated:

In 1437, England's Queen Mother, **Catherine de Valois**,[6] died, aged 35, in a nunnery. She had been sent there, in disgrace, after the royal family discovered that a few years earlier she had privately married a low-ranking Welsh royal servant, Owain Tudor. Together they had produced three sons and a daughter – all in secret!

6. *She was the widow of warrior King Henry V, and the mother of King Henry VI.*

' Wasn't that a
dainty dish to set
before the king? **'**

Traditional nursery rhyme

CHAPTER EIGHT

BREAKFAST IS SERVED

❦

Every four years since 1903,[1] the citizens of Landshut in Bavaria, south Germany, grow their hair long, put on medieval clothing, hide their watches, mobile phones and other modern gadgets, and spend three weeks partying. It's only fair to add that at the same time they are also working very hard, entertaining nearly a million tourists who visit their town to join in the fun. What are they celebrating?

---

1. *The pageant was originally staged every year, then at three-yearly intervals. It did not take place in wartime.*

A royal wedding, of course! To be precise, the marriage of Princess Hedwig of Poland to Bavarian Duke George the Rich. This took place in 1475, when their royal families joined together in a defensive alliance against Ottoman Turkish invaders. After the wedding, the newly married couple paraded through Landshut town centre. Ten thousand citizens waved and cheered, then tucked in to a lavish feast. Some details of that staggering wedding breakfast survive:

- **40,000 chickens**
- **1,500 sheep**
- **1,300 lambs**
- **500 calves**
- **320 bullocks**

The Landshut feast was generously paid for by the bridegroom's father. But often the cost of food for a royal wedding came out of the rather unwilling purses of the nearest nobles and peasants. In York in 1251, when Princess Margaret of England married Prince Alexander of Scotland, the citizens and local lords had to supply all the bread, 700 deer and 100 wild boar, while the archbishop of York provided 60 oxen.

But can you eat it?

At medieval public feasts, ordinary people stuffed themselves with bread, and with as much roast meat – a rare treat – as they could get hold of. But royal bridal couples and their guests enjoyed delicate, exotic fare such as roast swan, or prawns and porpoise. Medieval royal wedding banquets often ended with 'subtleties': little statues made of marzipan or boiled sugar (both very costly). Favourite subjects were lions, tigers, knights on horseback and unicorns; these featured, carrying 'confits',[2] at the wedding of Margaret of York to the duke of Burgundy in 1468. There might also be precious imported rarities, such as fresh sweet oranges.

Why 'wedding breakfast'?

No-one really knows. Unless the bride or groom are too nervous to eat or drink beforehand, it's not usually their first meal of the day. And traditionally, royal weddings were celebrated in the afternoon or evening. Some modern writers suggest that the word 'breakfast' survives from medieval times, when, following the teachings of the Church, bridal couples fasted before taking Communion as part of their wedding ceremony. However, there is no recorded use of the term 'wedding breakfast' until the 19th century. So perhaps it is a Victorian invention – like fish-knives.

2. *confits: sugared almonds or sugar-coated aromatic spices.*

Her Majesty's dinner

Food fashions change, and so have the menus served to bridal couples at royal wedding meals. These often included a dinner on the night before the wedding, given by the bride or groom's parents in very grand style indeed.

This was the menu for the dinner hosted by Queen Victoria, the evening before her son Prince George, duke of York, married Princess Mary (or May) in 1893:

Crayfish soup, royal style (with a garnish of little shapes made from savoury custard)[3]

✠

Salmon in caper sauce

Fried fillets of sole

✠

Pastry puffs filled with chicken, cocks' combs (ugh!) and cocks' kidneys, lambs' sweetbreads,[4] olives, mushrooms and truffles

Cold quails, coated in a rich, jellied sauce

3. *I am not making this up.*
4. *thymus glands — formerly a delicacy, now banned for human consumption because of the threat of BSE.*

❋

Braised beef with parsley sauce

Roast haunch of venison

❋

Ortolans – tiny force-fed songbirds (horrors!)

❋

Green peas cooked with butter

Cake soaked in syrup and brandy,
served with cherries

Meringues with cream, princess-style

❋

And on the side table:

Roast chicken

Boiled tongue

Cold roast beef

❋

Simple pleasures

Such extravagant, luxurious dishes were simply not available in 1947 when **Princess Elizabeth** married **Prince Philip**. Nor would they have been appropriate. Food rationing was still in force then for everyone in Britain – including the royal family. Mountains of rich fare would have been in very poor taste after so many people, in Britain and Europe, had suffered shortages during the 1939–1945 war. So the royal wedding breakfast was decently sparse and simple. Served to 150 guests (carefully chosen from the 2,500 who had been invited to the ceremony in Westminster Abbey), it had just three courses, plus fruit:

Fillets of sole, Mountbatten style

⚜

Partridge casserole
Green beans, roast potatoes, salad

⚜

Iced pudding 'Princess Elizabeth'
Sweetmeats

⚜

Fresh or dried fruit

I name this pudding...

Like many royal menus, Princess Elizabeth's wedding breakfast included dishes specially created by Palace chefs and named in the royal guests' honour.

Often the recipes for these were kept secret, but we do know that the 'Princess of Wales Chicken' served at the wedding of Prince Charles and Princess Diana in 1981 consisted of chicken breasts stuffed with a delicate mousse of lamb. Other dishes on offer at the same meal included light, fluffy brill (white-fish) dumplings with lobster sauce, and fresh strawberries with cream.

Also in keeping with changing times, rather than a formal meal after Prince Charles's second wedding, the Queen offered her guests a spendid selection of traditional British teatime finger-foods, including Prince Charles's favourite boiled fruit cake, specially made in Wales.

A piece of cake

No wedding, royal or otherwise, would be complete without a cake. 'Bride-cakes' (biscuits of barley grains and salt, symbolising fertility) are a tradition that dates back to Roman times, or earlier. Roman husbands broke their cakes over their new wife's head, for good fortune. Medieval couples kissed over a stack of them – the higher, the better. Later, royal wedding cakes copied this tradition, with tiers towering above the bride and groom, festooned with lacy sugar decorations, silver or porcelain ornaments, and garlands of flowers. The cake made for the petite duchess of York in 1923 was 9 feet (2.75 metres) high. It was decorated with church-like sugar arches, royal coats of arms, and tiny cupids holding wedding rings.

By around 1600, bride cakes had been replaced by 'bride's pies': minced meat, dried fruit and spices, all wrapped together in pastry. These eventually became the sweet, solid, dark, brandy-soaked, marzipan-coated fruit cakes favoured from Victorian times onwards. Such rich ingredients made them succulent and long-lasting, but also extremely heavy. The duchess's 9-foot cake weighed in at 800 lb (365 kg)!

In 2008 a piece of one of the 27 cakes made for **Princess Diana**'s wedding was sold, for charity, for £1,000.

In 2009 a slice of cake from the wedding of Queen Victoria's daughter **Princess Louise** (in 1871!) was offered for auction. It was then 138 years old – and potential purchasers were advised not to eat it.

In 2010 **Crown Princess Victoria** of Sweden – and her chefs – chose to break with tradition. Their cake was typically tall – 11 feet (3.3 metres) high – but light and very fragile. Its 11 tiers, made with mostly organic ingredients, were composed of almond meringue, chocolate crisp, champagne mousse and wild strawberries.

Very top table

Guests at all royal weddings are seated according to carefully worked-out plans, devised by palace staff with expert knowledge of protocol, precedence and diplomacy.

One of the most glittering seating arrangements of all time – even for a royal occasion – must have been at **Princess Elizabeth**'s 1947 wedding. Table No.1 was headed by King George VI, the bride's father, with his daughter at his right hand. Anticlockwise from them, the remaining guests were Prince Philip, Queen Elizabeth (the bride's mother), the king of Norway, Queen Mary (the bride's grandmother), the king of Denmark, Princess Margaret, the king of Romania, and Princess Andrew of Greece (the bride's new mother-in-law).

Tonnes of tins

After news of her forthcoming wedding was announced, Princess Elizabeth received many kind gifts from well-wishers wanting to contribute to the postwar wedding breakfast. As well as 500 tins of pineapple, the princess and her new husband also received a great many tins of salmon and countless sugared almonds.

Q. *Whose music was played at his own son's royal wedding?*

A. The late Prince Albert's chorale[5] 'This Day, with Joyful Heart and Voice' was played at the wedding of his son Bertie, Prince of Wales, in 1863.

Q. *Whose royal wedding breakfast included a 'bombe' – and a wedding cake made by the Army?*

A. Princess Anne's, in 1973. A 'bombe' is a frozen creamy dessert; Princess Anne's contained peppermint chocolate. The cake, made by Warrant Officer David Dodd, was as tall as the princess (5 ft 6 in/1.68 m).

5. *chorale: a choral arrangement of a hymn, usually simple enough to be sung by a congregation rather than a professional choir.*

' Now, nephew,
to your work!
Hey!
St George for England! '

*Typically ribald advice by England's
King Charles II, as his brother's
daughter, Princess Mary of York, and
her new husband, William III of Orange,
retired to bed on their wedding
night in 1677*

CHAPTER NINE

AND SO TO BED

The year was 1285; the place, Scotland. And it was a wonderful party! King Alexander III and his new bride, Yolande of Dreux,[1] were celebrating their wedding with a great feast, and music, and much merry-making.

But – oh no! Look! Over there – among the courtiers! How horrible! A skeleton – and it's dancing!

1. *Alexander's second wife; it was rumoured that in order to marry him Yolande had broken her promise to become a nun.*

Of course, the skeleton was a portent – and its ghastly warning proved true. A few weeks after the wedding, Alexander was hurrying home, keen not to miss a single night with his young, pretty wife. But it was dark, and the Scottish winter weather was, predictably, dreadful. Alexander – and his horse – lost their way, rode over a cliff, and were found, very dead, the next morning.

Celebrating in style

We do not know the precise details of Alexander III's wedding celebrations. But almost certainly, they followed a similar pattern to other medieval royal wedding days: first a splendid meal, with entertainments of all kinds (later weddings even featured experimental – and terrifying – weatherproof fireworks, as at the marriage of King Charles I's daughter, Princess Elizabeth, in 1613). Then, then, then – all this was followed by a ceremonial 'bedding'.

Royal razzle-dazzle

The marriage of teenagers **Mary, Queen of Scots** and the **Dauphin** (crown prince) of France, in 1558, was celebrated with jousting (at which a top nobleman lost an eye), a state ball, a procession through the streets (so that the bride and groom could scatter coins to waiting crowds), performances by hundreds of musicians, singers and dancers, and a second ball, where 12 gold and silver wooden horses pranced across the dancefloor, followed by mechanical silver ships that seemed to float along. These carried the newly-weds on an imaginary 'voyage of love' around the ballroom.

It was all very pretty – and extravagant. One wedding guest remembered that the magnificent jewels worn by the royal family lit up the room almost as powerfully as the flaming wooden torches.

Step this way...

But long before the feasting and dancing stopped, a royal bride was ceremoniously led from the room, surrounded by her female friends and servants. Laughing and joking, they helped remove her jewels and her heavy wedding dress.

Ceremonial undressing – and dressing[2] – could take a very long time; superstitiously, every single pin holding the dress and its trimmings in place had to be removed and thrown away. If a lady-in-waiting kept even one of them, she was doomed to remain unmarried for ever.

Then the bride's maids would dress her in a fine nightgown and perhaps a nightcap, and she would get into bed. In France, the honour of handing the nightdress to the bride belonged to the most recently married noble lady.

2. *As recently as 1947, it was reported that it took around an hour to clothe Princess Elizabeth in her beautiful wedding dress.*

Do us a favour!

Traditionally, royal – and ordinary women's – bridal gowns were trimmed with ribbons or rosettes. These 'favours' were designed to be pulled off or (more decorously) handed out after the wedding ceremony, and treasured as mementoes of the great event.

There was a most undignified scramble to snatch the blue bows taken from the pretty pink dress worn by **Catherine of Braganza**, wife of England's Charles II, in 1662. The poor bride was left with none for herself or her family.

By the 19th century, ribbons had been replaced by purpose-made favours:

At **Queen Victoria**'s wedding, guests were given delicate strips of silk decorated with crowns, lovers' knots, and the initials V and A.

In 1863, rosette-style favours printed with portraits of the royal bride (**Princess Alexandra of Denmark**) and groom (**Albert, Prince of Wales**) were worn by many onlookers.

In 1947, **Princess Elizabeth**'s and Prince Philip's royal wedding favours were tiny hand-tied posies of myrtle and Scottish white heather.

Bedroom business
(no, not that...)

The groom lingered longer at the feast, but, once his bride was ready, he also made his way to the royal bedroom. Usually he was accompanied by rowdy male friends, some musicians, and, of course, his most trusted male servants. After around 1750,[3] the groom would most probably bid them all a cordial goodnight, usher them out of the room, and then firmly close the door.

But for many centuries before 1750, the 'bedding' of royal (and ordinary) couples was a public ceremony. The idea that a bedroom was a strictly private space had not yet developed. Indeed, French and English kings regularly held *levées* ('rising-from-bed' audiences) when trusted advisors, servants and friends all met in the royal bedroom or dressing-room, to discuss state business with the monarch while he was washed and shaved and put his outer clothes on.

3. *or even earlier, if he were tactful and considerate like Charles I in 1625, when Henrietta Maria was in tears at the prospect of a public bedding ceremony.*

Royal four-poster beds had thick curtains all around – mostly for warmth and to keep out draughts, but they did provide some privacy. And even unmarried princes, princesses and nobles rarely slept alone. While on night duty, their servants were expected to doze on mattresses or truckle-beds in their masters' or mistresses' bedrooms.

Q. Which royal bride stayed up late to play the harpsichord on her wedding night?

A. Princess Charlotte of Mecklenburg-Strelitz, who married King George III in 1761. She entertained guests at the wedding feast by giving a song recital to her own accompaniment. The party finally ended at 3 a.m.

Goodnight, sweet prince ~ and sweet empress

However, wedding customs varied from place to place. Some public beddings were much more decorous than others:

In Denmark, at the wedding of **Prince Christian** and **Princess Magdalena Sibylla** of Saxony in 1634, the newly-wed couple were led together to the royal bed by 24 senior nobles. They were partly undressed – just a token gesture – and then served wine and chocolate (for that time, an amazingly rare and expensive luxury). After the royal couple had sipped these, they put their clothes back on and joined in the wedding party!

It was rumoured that extremely beautiful, but very highly strung **Empress Elisabeth of Austria** was so tired and nervous on her wedding night that she pretended to be asleep before her husband, Emperor Franz I, had even reached their royal bedroom. According to Austrian royal tradition he was led there not by his noisy friends, but by his *mother*…

Elisabeth had freely chosen the Emperor as her husband, but found marriage and royal court life very restrictive and lonely. Her beauty, charisma, sensitivity – and unhappiness – are sadly reminiscent of a certain 20th-century 'people's princess'.

Bless the bed!

Elsewhere, they did things differently. In France, for example, a bridegroom might be accompanied by a priest:

In France, in 1745, **Princess Marie Antoinette**'s bridal bed was blessed by an archbishop – and well sprinkled with holy water.

In Britain, the groom was likely to arrive together with a jovial cup-bearer. In royal – and ordinary – households, the bride and groom were traditionally offered a strengthening drink of wine[4] mixed with egg, sugar and stimulating spices (see page 178).

---

4. or whisky in Scotland, of course.

Rough music

After the priests and cup-bearers had departed, then, at last, it was time to leave the bride and groom together – to do their royal duty and create an heir to the throne. (And also, very likely, to have a private conversation with each other for the first time in their lives.)

But leaving the royal couple together did not mean leaving them in peace; guests often sang saucy songs or, like King Charles II (see page 160), shouted encouraging comments from just outside their bedroom. In some countries, well-wishers stayed there all night long. Or else, in Spain, they came back the next morning to inspect the royal bedclothes.

In 1493, **Doña Isabel** of Portugal married **Philip the Good**, duke of Burgundy. The sumptuous bed, specially constructed for their public bedding ceremony in Bruges, Belgium, was one of the largest ever made. It measured a record-breaking 12 ft 6 in by 19 ft 0 in (3.81 by 5.79 m).

Watching and waiting

In many countries, leaving the bride and groom together did not entail leaving them alone:

In 1533, when **Catherine de' Medici** wed **Prince Henri of France**, official witnesses followed French royal tradition and stayed in the bedroom. It was their task to confirm that the marriage… well, that it had become properly valid (see page 33).[5]

From a legal, diplomatic point of view, witnessing a royal wedding night was prudent practice. It avoided international political rows and embarrassing Church law-court cases of the kind that happened after English Prince Arthur's marriage to Spanish Princess Catherine in 1501.

5. Until the 20th century, many royal births were witnessed in a similar way. In 1930, the rather later than expected arrival of Princess Margaret (born in Glamis Castle, Scotland) caused problems for the British Home Secretary and other dignitaries, who had travelled there from London to be official witnesses – and who missed important government business while they waited.

The morning after his wedding, the teenage **Arthur** had boasted crudely to his manservant that he had spent the night 'in Spain'. But months later, after Arthur had died, Catherine swore a solemn oath that she was still a virgin. That information made it legal for Arthur's brother Henry VIII to marry her (which is what he wanted). Catherine – trapped without money, and surrounded by foreign courtiers – was powerless to refuse. But who could tell which version of the royal bedtime story was true?

Q. *Which ruler got bitten in bed?*

A. Emperor Napoleon of France, on the night he married Joséphine Beauharnais in 1796. Joséphine's pet pug-dog always slept on her bed, and resented the Emperor joining his new wife under the covers. Napoleon's leg soon recovered.

Right royal revulsion

Arranged marriages being what they were, some royal wedding nights did not go according to plan:

England's **King Henry VIII** had already been married three times when he wed **Anne of Cleves**. The next day, Anne reported to her ladies-in-waiting that he had kissed her, clasped her hand, and bid her a friendly 'Goodnight'. Henry himself was more outspoken. He admitted to Thomas Cromwell, his chief minister, that he had had neither the 'will nor courage'[6] for anything more.

In 1795 **George, Prince of Wales** married his cousin, **Princess Caroline of Brunswick**. When the Prince first caught sight (or perhaps caught a whiff) of his bride – who was famous for neglecting her personal hygiene – he had gasped: 'I am not well, get me a glass of brandy!' By nightfall he had drunk so much that his best man and servants had to support him as he staggered towards

6. By 'courage' he probably meant 'heart' (as in 'didn't have the heart for it') rather than 'bravery'.

the royal bedchamber. According to Caroline, George spent most of his wedding night in a drunken stupor, stretched out on the floor with his head in the fireplace.

But not quite all night, possibly. Again according to Caroline, who was scandalously indiscreet, as well as unwashed and immodest, the couple only ever spent that night and the two following ones together. Their daughter was born nine months afterwards.

After the couple had separated permanently, in 1796, Caroline had love affairs with several very unsuitable men – and was alleged to like dancing topless at parties.

> O gracious Queen, we thee implore
> To go away and sin no more.[7]
> Or, if that effort be too great,
> To go away at any rate.
>
> *Anonymous popular rhyme, c.1820*

7. *A paraphrase of John 8:11, which tells the story of Jesus and the woman caught in adultery.*

Happy honeymoons?

It is with some relief, dear reader, that we turn to the topic of royal honeymoons. For many medieval royal couples, these meant enjoying yet more dances, pageants, diplomatic receptions, tournaments and processions.

In 1565 Scottish religious reformer John Knox remarked, with extreme disapproval, about **Mary, Queen of Scots'** second marriage: 'For the space of three or four days, there was nothing but balling, and dancing and banqueting.' Mary – who was infatuated with her new husband, Lord Darnley – then spent the next few days of her honeymoon stirring up a political storm by (most unwisely) giving her bridegroom full royal powers as king.

All royal wedding celebrations, then as now, were accompanied by intense public scrutiny: 'What is she like?' On the day before her wedding, 16-year-old **Empress Elisabeth of Austria** (see page 168) compared this to being put on display like some kind of monster in a circus.

Since travel was unpleasant and often dangerous in earlier centuries, few royal honeymoons involved long journeys. So it is difficult not to feel pity for **Archduchess Marie-Louise of Austria**. In 1810 she had to spend her honeymoon with her husband, Emperor Napoleon, touring his newly conquered lands in cold, wet, muddy Belgium.

Even in the 20th century, a travelling honeymoon was sometimes not without its difficulties. In 1955, **Prince Rainier of Monaco** arranged a luxurious Mediterranean honeymoon cruise. But his new bride, **Princess Grace**, was seasick all the time.

However, a few royal honeymoons were spent happily, quietly – and (by royal standards) – in relative privacy:

In 1923, the shy, nervous **duke of York** and his bride (later **Queen Elizabeth the Queen Mother**) honeymooned first at a friend's country house, and then at remote, beautiful Balmoral. Though, sad to say, the bracing Scottish air could not stop the poor bride catching whooping cough.

Even the great **Queen Victoria** recalled happy honeymoon memories of simple, private pleasures: sitting quietly, watching Prince Albert shave, or letting him gently help her put on her stockings.

But – royal duty called! Victoria's honeymoon lasted just two days, at busy Windsor castle. Then, as she had already explained to Albert: 'My dearest love…I am the sovereign, and… [royal] business can stop for nothing.'

Royalty:
Privileged? Yes!
Pampered? Often.
To be pitied? Sometimes.

But never, ever – not even in bed – off duty!

A wedding posset[8]

1. Take a pottle (4 pints/1.4 litres) of cream, add one or two cinnamon sticks, heat until boiling, remove from heat and keep warm.

2. Take one pint/975 ml of sack.[9]

3. Beat together 18 small egg yolks and 8 egg whites, and 'mingle' them with the sack.

4. Add 12 oz/340 g sugar, a whole nutmeg, grated, and a little powdered cinnamon.

5. Heat the wine, eggs and sugar until hot but not boiling.

6. (This is the exciting bit!) Holding the hot cream as high as you can above the mixture, pour it on in a steady stream. Do not stir.

7. Sprinkle a little fine sugar, scented with musk and ambergris,[10] on top.

8. Cover the pot and keep it in a warm place until the posset has separated.

As the posset gently cools, it separates into three layers: creamy foam on top, rich custard in the middle, and a (very strong) spiced alcoholic liquid at the bottom. Enjoy!

8. *Based on a recipe in* The Closet of the Eminently Learned Sir Kenelm Digby, Knight, Opened *(London, 1669).*
9. *a very sweet fortified wine, like sherry.*
10. *traditionally sexy scents. Musk comes from the glands of wild deer; ambergris comes from sperm-whale guts (yes, really).*

Q. Who (according to Queen Mary) sent 'such an indelicate gift' to a royal couple?

A. Indian independence campaigner Mahatma Gandhi, to Princess Elizabeth and Prince Philip in 1947. In fact, his offering was perfectly innocent: a hand-woven cotton shawl. But many people mistook it for a loincloth, such as Gandhi himself wore as a protest against British rule.

Q. Which groom played 'hunt the carnation'?

A. Prince Maximilian of Austria, in 1477. Medieval wedding receptions often featured bawdy jokes and games. Maximilian's bride's mother whispered that her daughter had hidden a carnation somewhere 'about her', and that he must look for it. He found it in the bride's bodice.

Q. Which king got married in a monastery?

A. A community of celibate nuns seems an odd choice of venue for a wedding, but in 1254 King Edward I of England married his bride, Eleanor of Castile, at Las Huelgas monastery near Burgos in Spain. Their reason? Las Huelgas was very royal, as well as very holy. It had been founded by a Spanish ruler, and many Spanish kings and queens were buried there.

6 They [royalty] are
not people like us,
but with better hats.
They exist apart from
utility, and by virtue
of our unexamined and
irrational needs. 9

*'The Princess Myth: Hilary Mantel on
Diana': Novelist Hilary Mantel writes
about Diana, Princess of Wales in* The
Guardian, *26th August 2017*

CHAPTER TEN

NEEDS MUST

🦁

Well, royal hats sometimes can be really quite remarkable. Who can easily forget Princess Beatrice's flesh-colour uterus-and-tubes creation worn to William and Catherine's wedding? To be fair, Beatrice took all the jibes in very good part, and sold her hat on EBay to raise an astounding £81,100.01 for charity.

But that's rather missing the point...

The first edition of this book looked forward to the wedding of His Royal Highness Prince William Arthur Philip Louis of Wales, grandson of Her Majesty Queen Elizabeth II and second in line to the British throne (plus 15 others, in Commonwealth countries) to the more simply-styled and lowly-born Miss Catherine Elizabeth Middleton.

Now, almost seven years later, this new and expanded volume anticipates another UK royal marriage. We hope that Wills-and-Kate are happy, and that Harry-and-Meghan will be.

Naturally, any wedding should be a joyful occasion. But why (yet again) all the fuss? The millions of photos? The miles of print? The constant rumours? The endless gossip? And the knitting patterns? Yes, them as well. Last time round, Britain's *Daily Telegraph* offered loyal readers the chance to: 'Recreate the royal wedding in wool.'[1]

---

1. From 'Knit Your Own Royal Wedding' photo gallery on the Daily Telegraph *website*

We can't wait to see what kind of crafty ideas this latest royal wedding will inspire. Meghan is said to be a nifty calligrapher, and to have artistic interests.

Why the hoo-hah? Partly, because royalty sells. It attracts readers, viewers and advertisers. But there's more to royal weddings than souvenir tea-towels and battles for TV viewing figures. Somehow, we, the public, seem to need the royals and the grand occasions they stage for us, even if we deny it. Before Prince William's wedding, one in three Britons declared that they were not at all interested. However, when the day came (29 April 2011), well over half the British population watched at least part of the ceremony, along with countless millions in 180 countries, worldwide. And it's estimated – how?! – that the crowds cheering Will and Kate took 327 million photos between them. Clearly, a royal wedding matters to an awful lot of us.

If the royals didn't exist, we'd have to invent them. And, of course, we do. Over and over, all the time. To suit ourselves.

Keep in touch

'The genius of an event like this... is its simplicity, it's simultaneously magnificent and very simple.

And if the monarchy's going to survive, which in my view it will, it has to have that cleverness about a simple connection with everybody in the country.

However distressed and difficult the economic times are, it's essentially this mix between the informality and the public duty of the monarchy.'

Simon Schama, historian, commenting on Prince William's wedding in 2011

'If it made people feel romantic then that can't be a bad thing.'

Boris Johnson, MP. In 2011 he was Mayor of London

Good for business?

The royal family is the ultimate British brand, so it might be expected that a royal wedding would boost the tourist trade. Not so. In 1981, when Prince Charles married Lady Diana Spencer, the number of visitors to the UK fell sharply. The same happened in 2011. Presumably tourists wanted to keep away from the crowds.

On the other hand, a royal wedding is usually good news for souvenir sellers. William and Catherine's wedding boosted revenues for the Royal Collection to £41 million.

Bizarre bets

British bookmakers also love a royal wedding. In 2011, they offered the following odds to punters:

* 100/1 Prince Harry (William's best man) would drop the ring.

* 10/11 The Queen's hat would be yellow.

* 8/1 The Duke of Edinburgh would fall asleep during the ceremony.

Comparisons are always almost unfair, but William and Catherine were not the only royals to wed in 2011. For other royal couples, the experience was very different. Here are just two examples:

In Monaco, long-time bachelor Prince Albert III (53), perhaps the world's richest monarch, married striking, statuesque South African Charlene Whittstock, twenty years his junior. Both were Olympic competitors; her sport was swimming, his bob-sleigh. The couple reportedly met at a swimming gala. Just days before their wedding, it was also reported that a shocked and saddened Charlene was trying to flee the country, after hearing rumours that Albert had fathered another woman's child during their engagement.

The rumours were false, although Albert was already the father to two children born out of wedlock. As the Victorians might have said 'How different, how very different, from the home life of our own dear Queen'.[2] However,

---

2. *This remark was allegedly overheard during a mid-19th century performance of Shakespeare's* Antony and Cleopatra, *in London.*

the weddings (two: one civil, one Roman Catholic – the celebrations lasted 3 days) went ahead, and, in 2014, Albert and Charlene became the proud parents of royal twins – Prince Jacques and Princess Gabriella.

In Bhutan, the only nation officially to measure Gross National Happiness, Oxford graduate and Elvis fan King Jigme Wanchuck (31) married beautiful Jetsun Pema (21), art-lover, university student and keen basketball player. Respected for his diplomatic skills and genuine concern for his people, the King appeared very much in love with his bride, who he had first met when she was seven, at a picnic.

For their five-hour-long Buddhist wedding in a remote, historic monastery, the groom wore a robe patterned with roses and a raven (bird's head) crown embroidered with skulls. The bride wore scarves in five auspicious colours, and a headdress decorated with twin phoenixes, symbolising the blissful union between king and queen.

Dishes of traditional shamday (rice, potato and scrambled egg) were offered to the populace, so that they could share in the celebration. Later, in a tactful gesture towards Bhutan's Hindu minority, the new king and queen were married for a second time in a traditional Hindu ceremony.

Happy memories

Looking back, 2011 seems a long time ago. Grim news headlines then featured terrorism, international tensions and natural disasters. There was, as there always seems to be, a looming economic crisis.

Yet do we remember these unhappy facts in the same detail that we remember, say, the frocks worn by Catherine and her sister Pippa? Probably not. But why? Partly because images of those garments are still shown to us, repeatedly. But also because, on the whole, unless crises and disasters affect us personally, we prefer to look back to the past and remember happy events. Those don't worry or threaten us; on the contrary, they are reassuring.

So: yes, the frocks were pretty – even if Pippa's clinging gown provoked undignified 'rear-of-the-year' comparisons.[3] Those interested in the social significance of past textiles – a pretty rarified bunch, admittedly – might have wondered whether Carrickmacross lace, the immensely complex, delicate and laborious embroidery that inspired the decoration of Catherine's delightful dress, was perhaps the most tactful of options at a time of economic insecurity. Exquisite though its creations can be, the Carrickmacross technique was invented by a clergyman's wife in 19th-century Ireland and famously used to provide work for unemployed and starving young women after the tragic potato famine of 1846.

3. *Pippa Middleton was awarded this rather dubious honour at the end of 2011.*

Sniffers, Snipers, Spy Cameras

Not very romantic, but all are essential for a modern royal wedding. William and Catherine's was no exception. On 29 April 2011, 5,000 police officers (uniformed and plain clothes) were on duty. Thirty-five sniffer dogs checked the royal route. Marksmen and surveillance cameras were strategically positioned, and a police helicopter buzzed and whirred overhead. Armed bodyguards, disguised as footmen in powdered wigs and knee-breeches, accompanied the wedding cars and coaches. Seventy people, judged to be dangerous, were banned from central London, and anti-capitalists planning to behead royal effigies outside Westminster Abbey were arrested and moved away.

Thankfully, there were no serious disturbances. But ever since 1906, when the marriage of Spain's King Alfonso XIII to Scottish-born Victoria Eugenia was disrupted by assassins (the bride had to change out of her blood-spattered wedding dress before the ceremony could continue), when it comes to royal weddings, security forces across Europe have taken no chances.

Were you there?

The 2011 wedding guest list – 1,900 were invited – was supervised by William and Catherine themselves. It combined younger members of the Establishment with royal friends and relatives and a generous sprinkling of celebrities, from the Beckhams to Elton John. The comments were not always kindly: What on earth was 'so-and-so' wearing? Where was SamCam's hat? Would Victoria – very elegant though she looked – never, ever smile?

However, even though royal wedding guests saw[4] much less of the proceedings than those sitting comfortably at home watching on TV, an invitation – always sent by the Queen's Lord Chamberlain – was a great honour, and all of those invited seemed to be having a very good time.

---

4. *Westminster Abbey can seat around 2000; only 800 can see wedding processions moving along the aisle. Even fewer can see couples exchanging vows. Sad but true: the least important guests get seats with the worst views.*

Her Majesty's pleasure

After the service, the Queen held a reception for 650, at which 10,000 canapés, cooked by 21 chefs, were served (that's 15 tasty little mouthfuls per person). And champagne.

There was also, of course, a traditional wedding cake, decorated with 900 sugar roses, together with a rich chocolate refrigerator cake specially requested by William. American commentators calculated that a slice of each cake for each guest would have cost $133 (£99) to prepare and serve.

Then, in the evening, Prince Charles hosted a dinner with dancing for a select 300 guests. The menu was very British and organic where possible: salmon, crab and langoustine with herb salad; roast lamb with new potatoes and fresh vegetables; honey ice cream, sherry trifle and chocolate parfait.

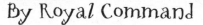

By Royal Command

According to former royal chef Darren McGrady, chocolate refrigerator cake of the sort served at Will and Kate's wedding was always a favourite at Her Majesty's tea-table.

It is said that the royal wedding edition used 1,700 biscuits and 17 kg of chocolate. Here is a smaller, simpler version:

200 g digestive biscuits, roughly crushed
200 g dried fruit (finely-chopped apricots are nicest)
300 g dark chocolate, broken in pieces
150 g butter
2 tablespoons golden syrup
Non-stick baking parchment OR greaseproof paper OR a little butter
Cake tin approx 20 cm x 20 cm (8 x 8 in)

1. Put crushed biscuits and dried fruit in large bowl. Stir to mix.
2. Line baking tin with parchment/paper or grease it with butter.
3. Melt butter, chocolate and syrup over very low heat. Do not boil.
4. When mixture is liquid, pour it over the biscuits and dried fruit. Stir well, so that all ingredients blend together.
5. Tip mixture into prepared baking tin. Smooth the surface.
6. Cool in refrigerator for several hours.
7. Cut into VERY small pieces to serve.

❛... the modern way is to marry someone you love....❜

HRH Crown Princess Victoria of Sweden, 2010

CHAPTER ELEVEN

IN LOVE, BUT OUT OF FASHION?

n the summer of 2017, Scotland's broadsheet *The Herald* printed a rather alarming news article. It reported that, statistically speaking, Scottish people were now more likely to develop cancer than to get married.[1] The institution of marriage is clearly in decline throughout Britain and in several other parts of the world.

1. 'Cancer diagnosis is now more common than getting married', The Herald, *10th July 2017*

Most of today's couples who do eventually choose to marry have dated for years, set up home and lived together before their wedding. William and Catherine first met in 2001, nine years before they announced their engagement, and reportedly became close companions a couple of years later. Apart from a separation in 2007 – during which cruel headlines sneered at Catherine as 'Waity Katie' – they have remained 'an item' ever since. So far, so normal, by modern standards.

Yes, but ....

In spite of the modern reluctance to get married, big, expensive weddings are growing in popularity among those who do choose to formalise their relationships. We all love a good party, but many weddings now seem contrived, controlled, choreographed occasions rather than old-style ceremonies with a jolly gathering attached. A whole new career has developed: wedding planner. And a surprising number of couples spend the equivalent of the average UK annual wage (£27,161 in 2016). Does every bride really want to be a 'princess' for a day?

Ultimate reality?

However, while most of us are not getting married, the merest hint of a royal wedding still sparks off a frenzy of anticipation. We still love royal romances. Why?

Do we see royals as characters in real-life soap operas or reality shows, providing public entertainment for free?

Are we living vicariously through royal weddings, enjoying frocks and flowers and music we could never afford ourselves?

Do we regard royal couples as symbols of continuity and renewal for our nation?

Are we all soppy, starry-eyed romantics?

Or are we just horribly, pruriently, nosy? Because – let's remember – we also feel free to comment, criticise, and dig up all the dirt we can discover about each royal couple. That's not nice ….

More middle than some?

Although invariably, snootily, labelled 'middle class' (it makes a nice alliteration with her surname), Catherine Middleton comes from a family with a standard of living that seems clearly above the norm. Her parents own a business and appear to enjoy a comfortable lifestyle. Thanks to an ancestor's trust, Catherine was educated at expensive private schools; only 6.5% of British children share that privilege. She went to a university where one in four students came from a wealthy background. After graduating, she had the use of a family-owned flat in a smart part of London. She is blessed by nature with intelligence, good looks and a charming smile. Little Miss Average she clearly is not.

Catherine's ancestors range from poor Durham miners and tough Tudor knights to prosperous Yorkshire wool merchants who married into titled families and occasionally entertained royalty. Further back, she is descended from a love-child of Henry VIII and – like at least 100 million[2] other people alive today – from father-of-nine English King Edward III (reigned 1327–1377). But when royal genes are scattered so far and wide, does 'appropriate' ancestry really matter?

2. Yes, really: Dr Andrew Millard at Durham University has calculated that there is an almost 100% probability that any modern-day English person with predominantly English ancestry is related to Edward III!

Who to choose?

In the past, royal brides and grooms were often complete strangers, who did not meet each other until the hour of their wedding. If love or respect or companionship later blossomed within rather than outside a royal marriage, then that was a bonus. Nowadays most modern royals can choose who to wed. And, interestingly, unlike their ancestors, they seem to prefer non-royal spouses – often with high-powered careers or, well, interesting backgrounds. Compared with some other young royals, Kate and Will seem rather tame by comparison, and even Meghan appears quite unexceptional.

Turn the page for a timeline of some modern royal marriages …

Some Modern Royal Marriages

1993
Crown Prince Abdullah of Jordan (since 1999 King Abdullah II) marries Palestinian Business Administration graduate Rania Al-Yassin. Queen Rania has won praise for her championship of education and international understanding.

1993
Crown Prince Naruhito of Japan marries diplomat Masako Owara. She refuses him, twice, before accepting his proposal, being understandably apprehensive about the stress royal responsibilities might bring.

1995
Crown Prince Pavlos of Greece marries British-American heiress Marie-Chantal Miller. After the marriage, she sets up a business selling high-class children's clothes.

2000
Prince Maximilian of Lichstenstein marries Panamanian fashion designer Andrea Gisela Brown. She is the first woman of African heritage – in modern times – to marry into European royalty.

2002
Crown Prince Willem-Alexander (since 2013 King) of the Netherlands marries Argentinian

economist Maxima Zorreguieta Cerruti. Maxima is intelligent and has a successful career; her father, well ... see pages 202–203.

2003
Prince Frederik of Denmark marries Australian marketing executive Mary Donaldson. They met in a Sydney pub; he introduced himself as 'Fred'. For a while, Mary did not know he was royal.

2004
Crown Prince Felipe of Spain (since 2014 King Felipe IV) marries glamorous journalist and TV news anchor Letizia Ortiz Rocasolano.

2011
Zara Phillips, Olympic medal-winning daughter of Princess Anne, marries England rugby captain Mike Tindall. Famously, he refuses to have his badly-broken nose set before the wedding so that it might look 'better' in the photos.

2013
Prince Felix of Luxembourg marries German bioethics researcher Claire Lademacher. She continues her studies after marriage in the sensitive area of organ donation.

2013
Princess Madeleine of Sweden marries American-British financier, Christopher O'Neill. He refuses a title – and Swedish citizenship – to continue his business career.

'Ma*b*e*l*gate'

In 2003, Prince Johan Friso of the Netherlands
anounced his intention to marry human rights
activist Mabel Wisse Smit. But the Dutch
prime minister refused to ask parliament for
the necessary permission, because the couple
had lied about the bride's earlier relationship
with a murderous drug-dealing gangster. The
wedding went ahead, in 2004, after Friso
gave up his right to the throne. Years later,
a security service official claimed that Mabel
had been a secret agent, working for the
Dutch government, at the time of her gangster
affair. True or false? Who knows?

On the face of it, the prime minister's reaction
was understandable. The dead gangster had
been the biggest crook in the Netherlands.
More upsetting – at least for the couple
concerned – was an earlier Dutch government
ruling on the wedding of Friso's brother
Willem-Alexander to Maxima Zorreguieta in
2002. The bride's father had been a member
of the dictatorship that ruled Argentina
from 1976–1983. He was banned from the
democratic Netherlands, and Maxima's

mother refused to go to the wedding without him. So neither parent was there.

Not only, but also...

Scandinavian monarchies, like Scandinavian societies, are generally liberal, but in 2010, King Carl XVI Gustaf and Queen Silvia of Sweden found themselves facing more than usually unconventional partners chosen by their children, Crown Princess Victoria and Prince Carl Philip.

It's not easy being a royal. After learning four languages, starting official duties aged only 18, studying at university, training as a diplomat, spending time with the army, and representing her nation at home and abroad, Victoria became stressed and unhappy and developed an eating disorder. As part of her plan to regain health and confidence, she went to a Stockholm gym – and fell in love with the owner, Daniel Westling.

As Swedish writer Sten Hedman neatly exclaimed: "She kissed her gym trainer and she got a prince."

Literally a boy from the backwoods , Westling was descended from Finnish foresters and subsistence farmers. He spoke with a country accent. His appearance was far from polished – scruffy even. He had no experience of public life. How could he possibly fit into refined royal circles, converse with ambassadors and statesmen, or support Victoria in all her royal duties. It was unthinkable!

But Victoria was determined. So was Daniel. He took lessons in history, tradition, etiquette, high culture, politics and languages. He got a new haircut, new spectacles and elegant new clothes. It took eight long years, but at last King Carl XVI Gustaf consented.

Victoria and Daniel were married in 2010. It was the biggest royal wedding since Prince Charles married Diana. But, in contrast, in the photos Victoria and Daniel both look happy.

However humble his background, Daniel Westling was clearly a 'respectable' person. But that was not what some people said about Sofia Hellqvist, whose close friendship with Victoria's brother, Prince Carl Philip, hit the

headlines shortly before Victoria's wedding to
Daniel.

Unlike Daniel, Sofia was no stranger to
publicity. In 2004, before she met her prince,
her photo had appeared in a leading men's
magazine, wearing only a bikini bottom – plus
a live python (or was it a boa constrictor?).
The next year, she took part in a TV reality
show, where she caused a sensation by kissing
a female porn star. But at the same time,
Sofia was studying, teaching yoga, and,
increasingly, working as a volunteer. In 2010,
she set up Project Playground, a children's
charity in South Africa, and since then has
devoted her energies to good causes. Bravely,
she is reported to have said: "I don't regret
anything. All these experiences have made me
the person I am."

In 2011, Sofia moved to live with Prince Carl
Philip in Stockholm; they married in 2015.

Do quit the day job

Most royal spouses have had to give up their former occupations, and sometimes, it seems, their previous identities. The reverse is not always true; like his grandfather, Prince Philip, William continued his service career for a couple of years after he wed. But then royal duties called.

Which royals were/are?

* Archaeologist
* Architect
* Marine biologist
* Army administrator
* Olympic sportsperson
* Furniture maker and designer
* Events organiser

Answers:

* Queen Margarethe of Denmark
* Prince Richard of Gloucester
* Emperor Hirohito of Japan
* The Duke of Kent, head of the War Graves Commission
* This one's easy – Zara Phillips, and her mother, Princess Anne
* David Linley (Lord Snowdon), son of Princess Margaret
* Peter Phillips, son of Princess Anne

Billy the fish or Just William?

Sometimes, occupations bring a change of name or title, even for royals. As sons of a prince, William and Harry are princes too. But while serving with air-rescue teams, William chose the modest 'William Wales'. This led to the nickname 'Billy the Fish' from his comrades.

Like all of Queen Elizabeth II's descendants, William's surname is 'Mountbatten-Windsor'. But, as a prince, he doesn't have to use it. Just 'William' (sounds like the classic children's stories) will do.

Even so, royal titles matter. At 8 a.m. precisely on the morning of his wedding, William also became, by gift of the Queen: the Duke of Cambridge in England; the Earl of Strathearn in Scotland; and Baron Carrickfergus in Ireland. As William's wife, Catherine shares his rank, surname and titles, in feminine form. It's rumoured that the Queen will make Prince Harry a royal duke – perhaps 'of Sussex' – on his wedding day, as well. So Meghan will become a duchess.

❝ Woman has baby ❞

*Cover of Private Eye (British
satirical magazine), shortly after
the birth of Prince George in 2013*

CHAPTER TWELVE

... AND THEN THERE'LL BE THREE!

Was it a hint? Was it coincidence? Was it a gracious, smiling 'thank you'? Or was it a sudden, unguarded, glimpse into the royal subconscious?

Whatever it was, Catherine's light-hearted remark when visiting Poland in the summer of 2017 opened the worldwide gossip floodgates. All she said, as she was handed the gift of a small cuddly toy designed to soothe fretful infants, was 'We'll just have to have more babies! But it was enough.

In consequence, the news of a third royal pregnancy, announced just weeks later, took few people greatly by surprise.

Really, why should it? Traditionally, royal families have been large. William's grandmother, Queen Elizabeth II, had four children. Her father, George VI, was one of six. Queen Victoria (1837–1901) had nine. Catherine and William are young and healthy and seem genuinely fond of children. Catherine has two siblings, and her family is said to be close and loving. Why should she not want to replicate her own happy childhood?

Even more important, and still even today, having babies is what royal women do – it's their royal purpose and their royal duty, especially if their husbands are likely to inherit a crown. Without them, the royal bloodline cannot continue; royal genes cannot be passed on. Their bodies are not just their own, but also a vital link in an ancient, if anachronistic, chain. They are following a well-rehearsed script, unwritten but inescapable.

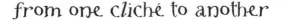

from one cliché to another

" In those days she [Catherine] was .... entirely defined by what she wore. These days she is a mother-to-be, and draped in another set of threadbare attributions. Once she gets over being sick, the press will find that she is radiant...."

Novelist Hilary Mantel, on reactions to Catherine's first pregnancy.

The more one thinks about the royal need to breed, the stranger it becomes. Biologically speaking, royal blood is no different from anyone else's. And, after all the marvellous advances in modern genetic science, does anyone still think that there is a mysterious force, essence or magic of royal-ness that can be linked to a particular pattern of chromosomes? No, of course not. Royalty is a property, like any other inherited status or title or estate. But it comes attached to an extraordinary burden of expectations and duties.

Royal by design?

Readers, your author is woefully ignorant of sci-fi books. So please excuse the following question: Has anyone written a story about what might happen if - or when - royal babies are genetically engineered to produce the perfect monarch for public consumption?

If they haven't, perhaps they should. It would make interesting reading.

Sickening

It must be horrid having your lightest remarks chewed over by all and sundry and even worse to have your medical condition discussed in detail in public. As the whole world knows by know, poor Catherine suffers from unpleasant, exhausting and potentially dangerous hyperemesis gravidarum (extreme sickness of pregnancy). Like any other woman with that condition, she deserves our sympathy.

Being sick is bad enough, but how must it also feel to have every visible pregnant movement recorded and scrutinised in the same way? Helped by hindsight, in September 2017 one British newspaper website printed three pictures of Catherine. Each showed her holding one hand lightly in front of her stomach in an instinctive, protective way.

One photo had been taken just after the announcement that Catherine was expecting her third child; the others dated from her previous pregnancies, two and four years earlier. 'Look, we can spy on Kate's most personal secrets!' was the photos' unspoken message.

Considering the countless millions of images of Catherine in circulation, how had journalists found the relevant pictures so quickly? Is all royal life now stored away in data banks, labelled and cross-referenced, ready for instant display to the public? For any ordinary individual, the thought is appalling.

'The most stylish celebrity tot'

Yes, that's what the headline claimed. Bizarrely, aged just three, Prince George had become a style icon. Although criticised by some for dressing her children in dated, 1950s style clothes, others have affected to find Catherine's choice of apparel for her son stylish and attractive. These garments are not cheap, however. A smocked shirt and shorts set, as worn by Prince George for his baby sister's christening, will cost doting parents or grandparents the best part of £100.

It's here! The great royal lentil shortage!

It seems that Prince George sets the style in healthy lunches, as well as toddlers' clothes. After he started school, aged four, at Thomas's in trendy Battersea, London, shops reported a sudden surge in demand for puy lentils – those peppery little grey-green pulses that are full of healthy fibre and don't go soggy when cooked.

Apparently, pupils at Thomas's are sometimes offered them for lunch, in a salad with smoked mackerel. A tasty combination, certainly, but perhaps, for ordinary mortals rather than princes, a little sophisticated....?

By the way, we don't know that George actually ate any lentils. But he was in the same building!

Not so funny

At the same time as George may, or may not, have been confronted by lentils, his school and his parents were facing a much more serious problem. A 40-year old woman, dubbed a 'royal superfan' by the media, was arrested after being found inside the school grounds twice within 24 hours. Some reports say she was attempting a burglary, others that she was 'besotted' by young royals. Either way it was alarming. After close questioning, the woman was formally cautioned by the police and warned to stay away from the school; if she obeys, she will not be subject to further charges. Security at Thomas's has been reviewed and tightened.

Short (well, fairly) and sweet

Compared with royalty from earlier centuries, William and Catherine have been rather restrained, and limited their choice of names to three each for their first two children:

George Alexander Louis, born 22 July 2013

Charlotte Elizabeth Diana, born 2 May 2015.

Nothing there to raise eyebrows or frighten the horses. Although Diana has painful memories for the royal family, the names themselves are conservative, pleasant and safe.

The new royal baby is not due until spring 2018, but there has already been keen interest in possible names. If it's a girl, the favourites are Alice, Alexandra or Victoria; if it's a boy, then Arthur or Albert are top suggestions. Wildcards for girls include Maud and Philippa; for boys, Phillip and James.

William and Catherine chose traditional names

for their first two children. But other young royal couples have been more adventurous. Among their offspring we can find:

Fashionable/popular: Oscar (Sweden), Noah, Liam (Luxembourg): Isabella (Denmark), Isla, Mia (grand-daughters of Princess Anne)

Religious: sisters Maria Laura, Luisa Maria and Laetitia Maria (Belgium)

Bound by custom: Christian (Denmark). For centuries, the first-born sons of Danish rulers have been called either Christian or Frederick. No other choice is possible.

Historic and heroic: Achileas-Andreas, Odyseas-Kimon (Greece)

Retro: Ingrid Alexandra, Sverre Magnus, Maud Angelica (Norway)

Neatly Matching: Amalia, Alexia, Ariane (Netherlands)

Tribute: Sofia (Spain, honour of mother-in-law)

Ethnic: Minik, Ivalo (a tactful choice of Greenland middle names for Danish royal twins Vincent and Josephine)

Unusual: Luana, Zaria (Netherlands), Savannah (granddaughter of Princess Anne).

But few people, royal or otherwise, can match the splendid collection of names belonging to one long-dead British prince: Charles Edward Louis John Casimir Sylvester Severino Maria Stuart, more usually, and succinctly, known as Bonnie Prince Charlie (1720–1788).

Work, work, work

Royal duties for newly-married princes and princesses, include more than just procreation. For all working royals, the job includes an awful lot of travel, and William and Catherine have attracted much international interest (or curiosity) – and many, many invitations. They were also ambassadors for the international Olympic Games held in London in 2012, and, like royals everywhere, are patrons of many charities. William also holds an honorary rank in the armed forces.

Royal wives, other lives

Naturally, it is an individual decision for each royal wife as to how much time she will devote to child care, how much to royal duties and how much to her own career. The balancing act can't be easy, but:

1. Who trained as a psychologist after she was married?
2. Who wrote a best-selling children's book about a peanut-butter sandwich?
3. Who campaigns for LGBT rights?
4. Who has 7 million followers on Twitter, and her own YouTube channel to win support for humanitarian campaigns?
5. Who is a United Nations Special Advocate for Inclusive Finance?
6. Who is a global ambassador for the Special Olympics?
7. Who claims to talk to animals and angels and put people in touch with the dead?

Answers:

7. Princess Martha-Louise of Norway
6. Princess Charlene of Monaco
5. Queen Maxima of the Netherlands
4. Queen Rania, again
3. Crown Princess Mary of Denmark (and also Princess Mette-Marit of Norway)
2. Queen Rania of Jordan
1. Queen Mathilde of Belgium

219

Enough is enough?

In July 2017, 'Having Kids', a campaigning organisation dedicated to encouraging smaller, planned families, wrote to William and Catherine to urge them to limit the number of their children.

In a statement, 'Having Kids' later said:

'William and Kate have a tremendous opportunity to model their choice of having a smaller family. By doing so, they set an example as to what has the most potential for mitigating climate change and its impacts, including severe flooding, deadlier heatwaves, increase in diseases, and wildlife extinctions….

'Moreover, given the vast economic inequalities in the world today, the couple also has the opportunity to model a simple principle: That every child deserves as fair start in life.'

The campaigners have some powerful arguments. However, as recent events have revealed, this time, they were probably just a litle bit too late.

Producing children has, for thousands of years, been a royal couple's prime duty. So being urged to stop by a charity, however well-meaning, might seem a little, well, inappropriate. But, also over the centuries, involvement with charities has been essential for royals young and old. Few, perhaps, have taken this so far as Prince Harry, who bravely took a public HIV test in 2016.

Charity is also one of the rare activities where royals are allowed to express genuine personal preferences. In the UK, William, Catherine and Harry co-ordinate their efforts through The Royal Foundation. Its favoured causes? Young people, sustainable development and the armed forces. Harry is also involved with Sentebale (Forget-Me-Not), which he founded in 2006 with Prince Seesio of Lesotho, to work with children affected by HIV/AIDS.

In 2017, Meghan passed her own charity test (of a kind), appearing for the first time as a couple with Harry at the Invictus Games. We wonder: which of the good causes she already supports will get added to the royal charitable list?

" Less is more, when
it comes to Royal
revelations.... "

Janet Street-Porter, Daily Mail
6th September 2017

CHAPTER THIRTEEN

THE PROBLEM OF PUBLICITY

ay back in the early 1970s, Princess Anne hit the headlines when she told a press photographer to 'Naff Off' – or more colourful words to that effect. Not long afterwards, she tried to explain how she felt about media attention:

"I accept all the press when on an official engagement as part of the scenery, but at horse trials the 'me' who does the official duties couldn't possibly ride a horse. It's a different sort of 'me'...."[1]

1. BBC/ITV broadcast, 13 November 1973

At a personal level we might sympathise; such constant scrutiny when doing something skilled and dangerous would surely try the patience of a saint. But Princess Anne's neat distinction between public and private royalty no longer exists – if it ever did, in reality.

For centuries, royal personages have controlled access to their private charmed circles, and tried, oh so hard, to manage their own images. Think of all those past royal portraits, carefully posed and composed. As an Art History major, Catherine Middleton must have studied some of them. Think of Elizabeth I, confounding critics of her spinster status with magnificent public rhetoric: "I have married England!"

Today, of course, the press and other media are so much more than Princess Anne's 'scenery'. They are uncomfortably locked together with royals, as part of the same story. Royalty now needs to win and keep the media on its side, just as much as the media needs a constant supply of 'news' about royal families.

In 2016, Catherine appeared, looking very glamorous, on the front over of the centenary edition of *Vogue* – the world's most influential fashion magazine. It was a great honour. But who was conferring the honour, and who receiving it? Royalty or the press? It is not easy to be sure.

Royal weddings are just one part – an important part – of this dangerous dance. A dance in which it's all too easy to lose touch with reality. Catherine must have understood what she was taking on when she married her prince. Life as a modern royal is materially luxurious, privileged, interesting, and full of experiences not open to others. It gives opportunities to exert influence and maybe even power. But it comes at a price – zero privacy, forever. Royalty's looks, actions, words and bodies are viewed as public property. Their entire existence is more circumscribed than most of us can imagine. It's gilded, right enough, but the cliché is correct. It's a gilded cage. Ever since their wedding, William and Catherine's life has been an unenviable balancing act. Duty or domesticity? Family or the royal firm? Them or us?

Don't overdo it

Looking back, Catherine and William's wedding, although lavish, seems pitched at a lower key than Charles and Diana's magnificent celebrations in 1981. Was this deliberate? Will and Kate's big day was a public holiday, but not a state occasion. Leaders of foreign governments were not automatically invited; there were no super-glam, superstar opera-singers performing. The bride and groom arrived in cars, not Cinderella coaches pulled by horses. And no-one dared mention the fateful word 'fairytale'.

Although a million London spectators sounds – and is – a lot, twice as many turned out to watch Charles and Diana. Why was this? Were William and Catherine not glamorous enough? By 2011, did fans of royalty prefer to experience everything on screen? Or did a temporary, pre-wedding lull in hostilities between press and palace mean 'no scandal = less interest'.

We could not be so cruel - or could we?

Perfectly unreal?

'Kate seems to have been selected for her role of princess because she was irreproachable: as painfully thin as anyone could wish, without quirks, without oddities, without the risk of the emergence of character. She appears precision-made, machine-made, so different from Diana whose human awkwardness and emotional incontinence showed in her every gesture...'

Novelist Hilary Mantel, 'Royal Bodies', *London Review of Books*, vol. 35, no.4, 21 February 2013.

Don't worry. That's not a criticism. Mantel is not discussing the 'real' Catherine, but her public persona: what royal advisors judged would be best to show us – and, perhaps, what we, the public, wanted to see.

It's so sad. Perhaps we'd like the real Kate even better – the actual person behind so many carefully-composed royal public images. But I expect the advisors are correct. We consumers of royalty can't be trusted. It would be too risky.

‘ She's just wild
about Harry! **’**

Vanity Fair *front cover,*
September 2017, below a picture
of actress Meghan Markle.

CHAPTER FOURTEEN

A WOMAN
WHO WORKS[1]

❧

I t was the dogs that let the cat out of the bag. As soon as it was reported that Meghan Markle was making arrangements to move her beloved 'rescue-pups' to Britain, it seemed obvious that she, too, was intending to make her home here. As if to remove any doubts, Meghan confided to a sympathetic reporter from US magazine *Vanity Fair*: 'We're a couple... We're in love... we're happy.'[2]

1. Meghan, on her blog: 'I've never wanted to be a lady who lunches –
I've always wanted to be a woman who works.'
2. 'Meghan Markle, Wild About Harry!' Vanity Fair,
September 2017

And so the stage was set. Even allowing for American lack of reserve, royal-watchers know that such public 'confidences' are rarely offered without careful forethought. An engagement was imminent, inevitable. The official announcement came on 27th November 2017.

This time, the wedding venue will be St George's Chapel, Windsor Castle. It's beautiful and historic but holds only 800 people, so, in royal terms, the wedding will be small-scale. The date will be in May; the royal family will foot the bill except for police and security. The ceremony will be religious; beforehand, Meghan will be baptised and confirmed as a member of the Church of England. She also plans to apply for British citizenship, and must already have paid over £1,000 for a 'family' visa giving her permission to stay in Britain.

Well, then. Back to the engagement. Did the nation rejoice? Yes and no. UK media, even the most staid, went into overdrive, presenting the flimsiest scraps of information as important news. Family, friends and political leaders offered congratulations – the duchess of Cambridge, Meghan's future sister-in-law, patriotically declaring that 'America's loss is our gain'.

From these warm wishes, we must except President Trump, who has refrained from comment. His opinions on the engagement are perhaps coloured by Meghan's reported description of him as 'misogynistic and divisive'.

Among the British public, some were 'thrilled and excited'; others didn't care. There were the usual complaints about the cost of the royal family to taxpayers, and the usual defences of constitutional monarchy in return. There were official photos – yes, Meghan is indeed very pretty, enviably slim and with legs like a gazelle – but oh! why such flimsy shoes, outdoors in dank November? Yes, the ring is impressive (and tasteful) too, and Harry's choice of diamonds 'from his mother's collection' is loyal, sweet and sentimental – though it also illustrates just how wide is the gulf between royalty-with-their-amazing-jewels and the rest of humanity.

Kiss and tell

Somewhere, in the middle of all this circus, was a real couple (one sincerely hopes) happily in love, submitting to ordeal by questions about their innermost thoughts and feelings on worldwide TV. He looked happy but apprehensive; she was smiling, articulate, reassuring.

Readers: none of us knows these people. Yet they tell us their secrets! It hurts no-one to learn that Harry proposed while the couple were cooking roast chicken, or that a mutual friend introduced them on a blind date in London in July 2016, or that they fell in love straight away because 'the stars were aligned'.

It's even rather disarming to be told that Harry – surely one of the most eligible bachelors on the planet – felt he had to 'up his game', because he was so impressed when he first met Meghan. But still, in these free and easy days, it's perhaps a little startling to be told that Harry and Meghan went away together – in a tent, alone, under romantic African skies – just three weeks after their first meeting.

In the same way, the couple's wish to use their collective fame and influence to try to make the world a better place was earnest, touching and utterly admirable. But oh, if only life and its problems, even for royals, were that simple.

Life and art

Engagements are meant to be happy occasions. And this one clearly was. But what are we to think when Meghan says that the first five or six months of their relationship was 'their time' – implying that the rest of their lives will be public property? Or when Harry enthuses about the rare, simple pleasure of a quiet, private supper together in front of the television? Perhaps we ordinary folks don't know how lucky we are. Or perhaps, for the world's most photographed prince and an actress who's pictured herself, her pets, her home, her food and her clothes on her own style website, life and public performance are already, inextricably, one?

When Harry Met Meghan

* July 2016
  Harry and Meghan are introduced by a friend.

* November 2016
  Royal advisors condemn the 'wave of abuse and harassment' that Meghan has faced from racist media.

* May 2017
  Harry and Meghan attend the high-profile wedding reception of Pippa Middleton.

* September 2017
  Reportedly, Meghan meets the Queen.

* September 2017
  Meghan's 'love story' interview in Vanity Fair.

* September 2017
  Harry and Meghan walk hand-in-hand in public at the Invictus Games in Toronto, Canada.

* November 2017
  Meghan retires from her acting career.

* November 2017
  The engagement is announced.

* November 2017
  Harry and Meghan perform their first public engagement as a royal couple, in support of World Aids Day.

Vive la difference!

Much has been made of the differences between Meghan and Harry: he's British, she's American; he's royal, she's a commoner. That's true, but the pair also have a surprising amount in common. Both:

* came from privileged backgrounds
* went to private schools
* had parents who divorced when they were children
* are fitness enthusiasts and love sport
* enjoy jet-set travel
* work with charities
* count powerful people and celebrities among their friends
* are rich – though Meghan has earned her fortune, while Harry inherited his.

Meghan is proud to be a 'strong, confident mixed-race woman'. Her father is of Dutch and Irish descent; her mother is African-American. Harry's 'English' ancestry includes Germans, Danes, Greeks, Scots and Welsh, together with Portuguese and North African. On his mother's side, he is descended from American, Irish, French, Scottish, English and Indian forebears.

Getting to know you

On the day their engagement was announced, Harry and Meghan admitted that they'd known little about each other before they met. Harry's early life and embarrassing faux-pas ('more army than royal', he explains) have been exhaustively publicised. But Meghan? Well:

* She was born in California, where her father was a lighting director in films and TV.
* Her mother is a therapist.
* Aged 11, she wrote to Hillary Clinton to complain about a discriminatory advert.
* She has a degree in theatre and international relations from Northwestern University.
* She has worked as a restaurant hostess, a calligrapher, and an intern in a US Embassy.
* She married film director Trevor Engelson in 2011 and divorced him in 2013.
* She collects art. She is a fashion trendsetter. She calls herself a foodie.
* Her 'The Tig' blog became (her words) 'an amazing community of inspiration, support, fun and frivolity'.
* In 2017 she campaigned to end the stigma around menstruation.
* She has supported One Young World, World Vision Canada, the Clean Water Campaign and the United Nations Political Partnership and Leadership Program.

fact and fiction

In 2014, during a visit by Catherine, real-life duchess of Cambridge, to New York, local children mistook her for Princess Elsa, storybook heroine of the blockbuster Disney movie, *Frozen*.

Will it be the same for Meghan? Will she slip through the magic mirror of modern media and emerge – at least for public consumption – as another fantastical blend of fact and fiction? Already, within hours of their engagement being announced, Harry and Meghan had been hailed as 'symbols of modern Britain'. In one sense that is true: one British couple in ten now identifies themselves as 'mixed heritage'. But in other ways, well... Almost all of us are not royal, and are not connected with royalty. And surely, as we read about royal brides and grooms and weddings through the ages, we really would not want to be.

So, Harry and Meghan – congratulations and best wishes! And also, to be honest, more than a few heartfelt commiserations...

Glossary

Alliance A political friendship or agreement.

Annulled Declared invalid.

Annulment A declaration (usually by a Church leader) on legal and religious grounds that a marriage was never valid.

Arrayed Richly clothed.

Asunder Apart.

Attorney A lawyer.

Betrothal A ceremony at which a couple make formal promises to marry each other at a future date.

Betrothed Formally engaged to be married, having made promises at a betrothal ceremony.

Bioethics The study of ethical (best, most beneficial) practice relating to biology and medicine.

Calligraphy The art of beautiful, decorative writing. A person who practises calligraphy is a **calligrapher**.

Caper A pickled flower-bud, used as a flavouring or food. It has a sharp, sour taste.

Cloth of gold Rich cloth (usually silk) interwoven with threads of metallic gold.

Commoner A person not born into a family of high social rank.

Confessor (as in 'Edward the Confessor') A person who proclaims and promotes the Christian faith.

Consanguinity Close family relationship (literally, 'shared blood').

Crown prince The eldest son (and heir) of a ruling monarch.

Dauphin The crown prince of France.

Dowager A widow who has been allowed to keep her late husband's rank and title.

Dower A gift of land, money or goods given to a bride on the morning after her wedding night.

Timeline of British monarchs
Don't know which British ruler reigned when? Look no further!

Kings and queens of England

• **House of Wessex**
829–839 Egbert
839–856 Æthelwulf
856–860 Æthelbold
860–865 Æthelbert
865–871 Æthelred
871–899 Alfred the Great
899–924 Edward the Elder
924–939 Æthelstan
939–946 Edmund
946–955 Eadred
955–959 Eadwig
959–975 Edgar
975–978 Edward the
Martyr (honoured as a
saint by some)
978–1013 Æthelred the
Unready

• **House of Denmark**
1013–1014 Sweyn
Forkbeard

• **House of Wessex**
1014–1016 Ætheldred the
Unready (again)
1016 Edmund Ironside

• **House of Denmark**
1016–1035 Cnut the Great
1035–1040 Harold
Harefoot
1040–1042 Harthacnut

• **House of Wessex**
1042–1066 St Edward the
Confessor
1066 Harold

• **House of Normandy**
1066–1087 William I,
the Conqueror
1087–1100 William II
1100–1135 Henry I
1135–1154 Stephen
(disputed with Matilda, in
power 1141)

• **House of Plantagenet**
1154–1189 Henry II
1189–1199 Richard I,
the Lionheart
1199–1216 John
1216–1272 Henry III
1272–1307 Edward I

1307–1327 Edward II
1327–1377 Edward III
1377–1399 Richard II

• **House of Lancaster**
1399–1413 Henry IV
1413–1422 Henry V
1422–1461 Henry VI

• **House of York**
1461–1470 Edward IV

• **House of Lancaster**
1470–1471 Henry VI
(again)

• **House of York**
1471–1483 Edward IV
(again)
1483 Edward V
1483–1485 Richard III

• **House of Tudor**
1485–1509 Henry VII
1509–1547 Henry VIII
1547–1553 Edward VI
1553 Jane Grey
(disputed)
1553–1558 Mary I
1558–1603 Elizabeth I

• **House of Stuart**
1603–1625 James I
of England and
VI of Scotland
1625–1649 Charles I

• **Interregnum**
1649–1660
Commonwealth and
Protectorate period – no
ruling monarch

• **House of Stuart**
1660–1685 Charles II
1685–1688 James II
of England and
VII of Scotland
1689–1702 William III,
co-ruler with:
1689–1694 Mary II
1702–1707 Anne
(subsequently queen
of the United Kingdom,
1707–1714)

Index

Monarchs are English or British unless otherwise stated

Kings and queens of the United Kingdom

- **House of Stuart**
1707–1714 Anne

- **House of Hanover**
1714–1727 George I
1727–1760 George II
1760–1820 George III
1820–1830 George IV
1830–1837 William IV
1837–1901 Victoria

- **House of Wettin (Saxe-Coburg-Gotha)**
1901–1910 Edward VII

- **House of Windsor**
1910–1936 George V
1936 Edward VIII
1936–1952 George VI
1952–present Elizabeth II

Rulers of Wales

From the time the Romans left the British Isles (around AD 400) until almost 1,000 years later, the rugged land of Wales was controlled by many local rulers, often with the title of 'prince'. Few of them claimed to be national kings, like their neighbours in England and Scotland. But some of the most powerful did control most of Wales. They included:

844–878 Rhodri the Great
916–942 Idwal the Bald
942–250 Hywel the Good
1055–1063 Gruffydd ap Llywelyn
1155–1197 Rhys ap Gruffydd
1195–1240 Llywelyn the Great
1246–1255 Owain the Red

1246–1282 Llywelyn the Last
1372–1378 Owain of the Red Hand (exile)
1400–1416 Owain Glyndŵr

Kings and queens of Scotland

• **House of Alpin**
834–858 Kenneth I
858–862 Donald I
862–877 Constantine I
877–878 Aed
878–889 Eochaid and (perhaps) Giric
889–900 Donald II
900–943 Constantine II
943–954 Malcolm I
954–962 Indulf
962–967 Dubh
967–971 Cuilen
971–995 Kenneth II
995–997 Constantine III
997–1005 Kenneth III
1005–1034 Malcolm II

• **House of Dunkeld**
1034–1040 Duncan I
1040–1057 Macbeth
1057–1058 Lulach
1058–1093 Malcolm III Canmore
1093–1097 Donald III (1094 Duncan II)
1097–1107 Edgar
1107–1124 Alexander I
1124–1153 David I
1153–1165 Malcolm IV
1165–1214 William I
1214–1249 Alexander II
1249–1286 Alexander III

• **House of Fairhair**
1286–1290 Margaret of Norway (never crowned)

• **Kingdom disputed**
1290–1292

•**House of Balliol**
1292–1306 John de Balliol

• **House of Bruce**
1306–1329 Robert I, the Bruce
1329–1371 David II

• **House of Stewart (Stuart)**
1371–1390 Robert II
1390–1406 Robert III
1406–1437 James I
1437–1460 James II
1460–1488 James III
1488–1513 James IV
1513–1542 James V
1542–1567 Mary I (Mary, Queen of Scots)
1567–1625 James VI of Scotland and (from 1603) I of England

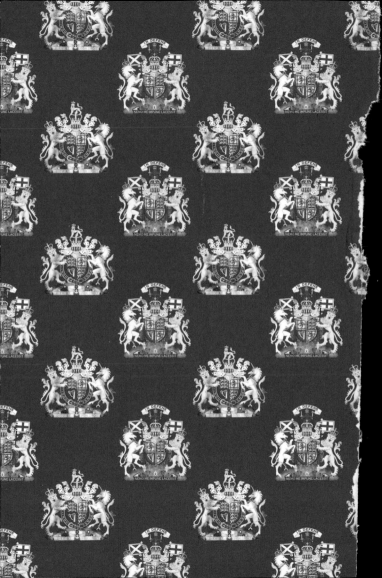